Albert Einstein

Albert Einstein

GENIUS OF THE TWENTIETH CENTURY

ALLISON LASSIEUR

FRANKLIN WATTS
A Division of Scholastic Inc.
New York Toronto London Auckland Sydney
Mexico City New Delhi Hong Kong
Danbury, Connecticut

Photographs © 2005: AIP Emilio Segre Visual Archives: 49 (Gezari Collection), 9 (The Hebrew University of Jerusalem, Einstein Archives), 78 (Library of Congress), 38, 102; akg-Images, London: 11, 34, 72; AP/Wide World Photos/Mati: 62; Courtesy of the Archives, California Institute of Technology: cover portrait (Anton Schaller), 88 (Robert Seares); Corbis Images: 6, 82 (Austrian Archives), 17, 40, 65, 91 (Bettmann), 56, 77 (Hulton-Deutsch Collection), 110 (Hanan Isachar), 63 (Tom Rogers/Reuters), 30, 32, 94, 108 (Underwood & Underwood); Getty Images: 2, 107 (Esther Bubley), cover background, 53 (Roger Viollet); Hulton | Archive/Getty Images: 86; ImageState: 45; Peter Arnold Inc./Popperfoto/Bilderberg: 98; The Image Works/Topham: 51 (Keystone), 43 (PA), 48 (Science Museum, London/HIP), 8, 15, 24, 35, 69, 90, 106; Time Life Pictures/Getty Images/March of Time: 100.

Library of Congress Cataloging-in-Publication Data

Lassieur, Allison.
    Albert Einstein : genius of the twentieth century / Allison Lassieur.— 1st ed.
        p. cm. — (Great life stories)
    Includes bibliographical references and index.
    ISBN 0-531-12401-0
    1. Einstein, Albert, 1879–1955—Juvenile literature. 2. Physicists—Biography—Juvenile literature. I. Title. II. Series.
    QC16.E5L345 2005
    530'.092—dc22
                                                                                        2004014313

Contents

Albert Einstein was born in Ulm, Germany, in 1879.

Early Years

The small southwestern German city of Ulm lies on the banks of the Danube River in the foothills of the Swabian Alps. In 1879, it was a bustling town with shops, homes, and small businesses. Life in Ulm was happy and comfortable for one shopkeeper, Hermann Einstein, and his wife, Pauline.

On March 14, Pauline gave birth to the couple's first child, a son. They were overjoyed and named their little boy Albert. But their joy turned to alarm when they saw that their new baby's head was large and misshapen. The doctor assured them that over time, the baby's head would become normal. Sure enough, after several months, little Albert's head looked normal.

THE EINSTEIN FAMILY

Albert Einstein was born into a family of Jewish Germans. Members of both his parents' families had lived in the Swabian region for years. Many of them had been merchants and shopkeepers. Hermann Einstein's father, Abraham Einstein, had been a merchant. Pauline's father, Julius Koch, owned a very profitable grain business.

Hermann Einstein was a kind, good-natured man who was loved and respected by his family and friends. When Albert was born, Hermann had a business selling goose feathers for bedding. It was not a glamorous job, but it was honest work that could support his new family. He was known as a hardworking person, but he always found time to enjoy his family and to take vacations into the countryside.

Hermann's wife, Pauline, was a lively, intelligent woman who loved music and art. She played the piano and read literature. Pauline took education very seriously and made sure that Albert and his sister Maja, who was born two years later, got the best education possible. She and her husband created a stable, loving home for their children. Hermann and Pauline shared a casual view of their religion. They respected their

Albert's father, Hermann Einstein, had a business selling goose feathers while his mother, Pauline, looked after the children.

Birthplace of a Future Genius

When Albert was born, it was normal for women to give birth in their homes. The Einsteins welcomed little Albert into the world in their apartment in Ulm. The family moved when Albert was only a year old, so he had no memories of his birthplace. The building was later destroyed. Years later Albert was shown a photo of the house before it had been destroyed. He is thought to have said, "Time has affected it even more than it has affected me."

Today a sign marks the place where the building once stood. Tourists still travel to Ulm to see the spot where Albert Einstein was born.

Jewish heritage but did not practice their faith. The family did not attend synagogue or pray in their home. Albert grew up knowing about his faith but not practicing it in any serious way.

Although many of Albert's relatives lived in Germany, other members of his parents' families had settled in other areas, including Italy and Belgium. Members of Albert's extended family maintained close ties to one another. As Albert grew up, he came to understand that he could rely on his family to help him if there was ever a need. This instilled in him a sense of duty to help others that remained with him for his entire life.

GOODBYE TO ULM

Sometime during Albert's first year, Hermann's youngest brother Jakob came to visit the family in Ulm. Jakob was an engineer who owned a small water and gas installation business in the city of Munich. Jakob convinced Hermann that there were wonderful business opportunities in Munich. The city held unlimited possibilities, Jakob explained, for two ambitious brothers to make money. Hermann agreed. He decided to close his feather business and become Jakob's partner in Munich.

When Albert was one year old, the Einstein family moved to Munich. They eventually settled in a large house in the outskirts of the city. The home had a lovely garden filled with shady trees—just the thing for a growing family.

The new business was successful. Jakob oversaw the technical matters while Hermann took charge of the commercial aspects. Later they added electrical engineering to the business. At that time, electricity was a new and exciting technology. People were anxious to install electric lighting in their homes and businesses. The future looked bright for the Einstein family.

A BRIGHT AND UNUSUAL CHILD

When Albert was very young, his parents were worried that he was developing more slowly than other children. According to Albert, he didn't begin to talk until he was about three years old. His parents were so worried about this that they consulted a doctor.

The way little Albert spoke to people was a cause of great concern. If someone asked him a question, for instance, he would first think of the answer, then try it out under his breath. Then, if he was satisfied with his response, he would say it aloud. Einstein later recalled that he spoke this way because he was determined to speak in entire sentences. Unfortunately, some people interpreted this slowness as proof that Albert was not very smart. In fact, it showed how thoughtful and deliberate he was.

Albert's sister Maja was born when he was about two years old. They became very close and remained good friends throughout their lives. During the first few years of his life, Albert was a

Albert and Maja were only two years apart in age and were close friends.

temperamental child, prone to tantrums and fits of anger. Maja learned very quickly to get out of Albert's way when he was angry. According to her, his face changed color when he became furious. Many years later Maja remembered Albert's rages and remarked that a sound skull was needed to be the sister of a thinker.

When he was five years old, Albert had an experience that hinted at the thinker he would become. He was home sick in bed, and his father gave him a small pocket compass to keep him amused. The young boy was intrigued by the compass. He played with it for a long time, turning it and shaking it, watching the needle always point north. He tried to puzzle out what invisible force was at work on the compass. The compass made a lasting impression on Albert. Many years later he recalled the day, saying that playing with the compass had made him realize that the behavior of the needle meant that something deeply hidden had to be behind things. Later he described this experience as being the first "wonder" of his childhood.

Albert Falls in Love with Music

When Albert was six years old, his mother insisted that he learn to play the violin. She wanted to share her passion for music with her son, so she bought him an instrument and hired a private teacher. Albert hated the lessons, but his mother forced him to continue them. Much later he admitted that it was the memorization he hated, not the music itself. When he was allowed to play real music, such as works by Mozart and Beethoven, he fell in love with the violin. He continued to play throughout his life. As an adult, it was normal for Albert to ask his friends to join him in playing duets.

School Years

At age six, Albert started school. Usually, Jewish children attended Jewish schools. Hermann and Pauline decided to send Albert to a nearby Catholic school instead. He was required to take religion classes in which he learned stories from the Christian scriptures and the beliefs of the Catholic faith. But rather than making him feel uncomfortable, Albert enjoyed the classes. He learned that there were many similarities between Catholicism and Judaism.

Albert was a thoughtful child who never gave a quick answer to a question. He knew that the teachers punished students who gave wrong answers with a whack of a ruler on the knuckles, so he always tried to have the right answer. He thought about the question, mouthing the words to his response slowly before answering. After he answered, Albert might move his lips as he repeated the words again to himself. This behavior made some teachers think that he was mentally challenged.

Albert received good grades during his first few years of school, but he eventually began to resist the way that teachers taught. Albert felt that school was very much like the military, with rigid rules. Albert made no effort to study subjects that bored him, so he did poorly in those subjects. However, he did well in any subject that captured his interest. By the time he was about eight years old, after two years in elementary school, Albert showed talent in math and Latin. He ignored all his other subjects, which made some of his teachers think that he was stupid.

Albert didn't fare much better with his fellow students. No one cared that he was Jewish, and he never felt out of place in the Catholic school because of his religion. However, he was a loner who did not like to play sports, and the other children considered that strange. Albert spent most of his early school years by himself.

ALBERT DISCOVERS THE EXCITING WORLD OF MATH

Hermann and Pauline Einstein did continue to observe one Jewish tradition: inviting a poor Jewish student to lunch once a week. The Jewish

"A Merry Science"

Albert's love of mathematics was inspired by his Uncle Jakob. His uncle made learning math into a game. He gave Albert tricky math problems to solve and used funny stories to introduce Albert to algebra. Uncle Jakob called algebra "a merry science" and said solving algebra problems was like going hunting for a little animal whose name is not known, so it is called *x*. These stories made Albert excited about math.

student who came to Albert's house each Thursday for lunch was Max Talmey, a medical student. Max immediately saw how intelligent Albert was and began bringing the boy books about science and math. Albert absorbed this knowledge with excitement. He read the books that Max brought and looked forward to their Thursday discussions.

Albert thrived in this learning environment. He could study at his own pace and absorb as much information as he wanted. He grew to like school even less.

TROUBLE IN SCHOOL, HAPPINESS AT HOME

Albert entered the Luitpold Gymnasium when he was ten years old. The gymnasium was a secondary school that taught a variety of subjects, such as math, science, languages, geography, and literature. Albert hated his new school as much as he had hated elementary school. The teachers still expected the students to be quiet and obedient in class. Albert chafed at these restrictions. He continued to answer questions slowly and deliberately, which did not make him very popular with the teachers.

Albert hated a lot of his classes in school, but loved tackling mathematical problems and learning theories.

One bright spot in Albert's life was learning a new type of math called geometry. Geometry is a branch of mathematics that studies points, lines, angles, curves, surfaces, and solids. When Albert was twelve years old, Max Talmey gave him a book of geometry. Albert began working through the book on his own, solving the problems and making notes. Geometry amazed and delighted Albert. He would later refer to the book as the "sacred little geometry book." Geometry was the perfect subject for Albert, because he could think through a problem step by step and come to a concrete, sure answer. Soon Albert was so good in math that he had surpassed Max in knowledge of the subject.

A HIGH SCHOOL DROPOUT

While Albert was struggling in school, his father's business was failing, mainly because of competition. By the time Albert was fifteen, the Einsteins' electrical business was nearly bankrupt. Pauline's family members, who were living in Italy, offered to help. They had only one demand, however. The Einstein family had to move to Italy. Albert had one more year left of school before he graduated. The family decided to accept the offer and move to Italy, leaving Albert behind in Munich to finish school.

Albert moved into a boardinghouse. He began to dread school even more. Albert's continued dislike of sports made him an outcast among the other students. Most of his teachers disliked him as well. One teacher even told him that he would never amount to anything.

Albert missed his family terribly. School was torture. He became depressed and ill. He asked a doctor to sign a certificate saying that he was suffering from exhaustion. His math teacher, one of the few teachers who liked Albert, then wrote a letter saying that Albert had learned everything about math that he could be taught at the school. The school officials were happy to release him. Albert was a high school dropout.

Albert begged his father to help him renounce his German citizenship at this time. His father seems to have ignored his son's request, but it was clear that Albert was anxious to leave all traces of his unhappy life in Germany behind him.

ALBERT FLUNKS AN IMPORTANT TEST

Soon Albert headed for Milan, Italy. For a time, Albert rested, loafed, and visited museums. He also read some of the popular science literature of the time. He made new friends, and they explored the beautiful Italian countryside together.

Albert's father, however, was not happy with Albert's newfound freedom. Hermann was working hard to get a new business started and

Albert enjoyed exploring the city of Milan after he left school.

pushed Albert to get a job. Albert refused to consider it. He couldn't imagine himself being chained to a boring job. However, he had ruined his chances of earning a university degree that would lead to a stimulating job when he dropped out of high school. Tensions ran high in the Einstein household for a time.

Finally, Hermann convinced the reluctant Albert to go back to school. Albert decided to apply to the Swiss technical college, Zurich Polytechnic. Its biggest advantage was that Albert only needed to pass an entrance exam to be accepted. He didn't need a high school diploma. Albert also agreed to help out with the family business. For several months Albert divided his time between studying for the entrance exam and working in his father's business.

Everyone was sure that Albert would pass the test easily. But Albert failed. His dislike of studying subjects that bored him was his downfall.

First Love

Because Albert's home was far away from Aarau where he went to school, he stayed with the family of Jost Winteler, a teacher at the school. Winteler had a young daughter named Marie. Albert and Marie fell in love. Many of their letters have survived, revealing the first love of Albert's life.

Some of Albert's letters to Marie were filled with silly, affectionate names for her, such as "my dear little sunshine" and "beloved sweetheart." But the sweet letters from Albert stopped when he started attending school at the Polytechnic. Marie was confused. She had no idea that Albert had met someone else, a serious classmate named Mileva.

He scored poorly on most of the test. However, he earned very high scores on the math and science sections.

Albert and his family were bitterly disappointed. But the professors at the Polytechnic noticed Albert's aptitude for science and math. They also saw that Albert was two years younger than most students who took the test. They decided to let Albert into the school the following year without taking the exam again. However, he had to have a high school diploma. Albert became determined to get a high school education.

ALBERT THE DROPOUT FINALLY GRADUATES

The Einstein family found a high school for Albert in the town of Aarau, near the Swiss–German border. At first Albert was apprehensive about going to another high school. However, he soon discovered that this school was much different from his last. The teachers were casual and friendly. They encouraged the students to discuss their studies and other topics, such as politics.

Albert loved his new school and was soon earning very good grades. He was allowed to focus his studies on the subjects that he had flunked on the Polytechnic entrance test. He also took violin lessons. At the end of his year in Aarau, Albert easily earned his high school diploma. So, in the fall of 1896, Albert began his studies at the Zurich Polytechnic.

THREE

Einstein Struggles for a Career

During Albert Einstein's year in Aarau, he had begun to explore areas of science and math that interested him. He was drawn to a branch of study known as physics, which is the science of matter and energy and how they interact with one another. For Albert, understanding physics seemed to be the key to understanding greater questions about the world.

TROUBLE AT POLYTECHNIC

Albert's plan was to attend Polytechnic for four years, studying to become a teacher. He studied many subjects, including math, physics, astronomy, and geology, which would prepare him to become a science teacher. He also took other classes, including business and philosophy, because they interested him.

Even in college, Albert continued to do well in the subjects that interested him and to ignore those that didn't. Once again, some of his teachers began to dislike his casual attitude and his habit of skipping classes he didn't care for. For example, Albert had a habit of addressing his physics professor as "Herr [Mr.] Weber" rather than the more formal and respectful "Herr Professor." Albert's math professor called him a "lazy dog."

When Albert was not in class, he used much of his time to study on his own. He read constantly, usually physics and philosophy books. In this way Albert continued his education, although many of his professors would have preferred that he attend their classes instead.

First Glimpse of a Brilliant Mind

In the summer of 1895, when he was sixteen years old, Einstein wrote a paper titled "Examination of the State of the Ether in the Magnetic Field." It was a brief, five-page overview of everything he had learned about electricity, magnetism, and a substance then known as ether. At the time, scientists believed that ether was a substance that filled all of space. Most of what Einstein wrote in his paper was information that was commonly understood at the time. But the paper was a remarkable first attempt by a teenaged Einstein to form and express his ideas about science. He sent a copy of this paper to his favorite uncle, Uncle Caesar, his mother's brother.

Because Albert's father's business was not doing well, Albert was forced to live on very little money. He rented a small room near the university. His mother's family gave him a small allowance. For entertainment, Albert often played his violin and attended free concerts. He saved part of the money he was given so that he could one day pay the fees that were required to become a Swiss citizen. Albert was still determined to renounce his German citizenship.

FORGING LIFELONG FRIENDSHIPS

Albert made a few close friends while attending Polytechnic. Two of them were fellow students Marcel Grossmann and Mileva Maric. Michele Besso also became a friend. Albert remained close friends with these three people for years. They frequently debated political issues and discussed physics and philosophy with him. Albert found them to be a source of great support throughout his school years. Marcel helped Albert pass tests by giving him his notes to lectures that Albert had skipped. Years later Einstein acknowledged that he didn't know how he would have graduated without Grossmann's help.

Mileva Maric was of Serbian heritage, and her family lived in an area of what was then Hungary. Mileva was intelligent, witty, and open minded. She was a courageous young woman in that she was determined to get a good education despite the fact that few women were allowed access to higher learning at that time. There were no universities open to her in her native country, so she traveled to Switzerland to attend Polytechnic. She was the only woman in her class.

Albert and Mileva became friends and gradually fell in love. When they returned to their families for school vacations, they wrote loving letters to one another. Once, Albert carried Mileva's picture home with

Einstein fell in love with another student, Mileva Maric. His family and friends didn't understand his attraction to her.

him to show his mother and sister, who teased him about his new girlfriend.

At that time Albert was a good-looking young man with intense eyes and a serious, yet humorous nature. His friends and family couldn't understand why he was attracted to Mileva. She often had a dour and gloomy air about her. Albert's friends didn't think she was very attractive. A childhood ailment had left her with a lifelong limp. But Mileva and Albert shared the same fascination with physics and had similar views on politics and culture. They thought of themselves as a team and dreamed that they would one day make tremendous discoveries in science together. They planned to get married as soon as they graduated Zurich Polytechnic and found jobs as teachers. Both of them were confident and happy with their plans for the future.

BAD NEWS FOR ALBERT AND MILEVA

In 1900, Albert and Mileva took the final exam to graduate from Zurich Polytechnic. Once again, Albert was in trouble. He hadn't studied much or attended class and was in real danger of flunking once again. His friend Marcel Grossmann came to the rescue, helping him study and giving him all of his own notes. When the results were posted, Albert had passed, but his marks were not high.

Mileva failed the test and was bitterly disappointed. She could not become a teacher until she had passed the exam. Einstein encouraged her to return to school and try again the next year, and she agreed. She returned to her family while he looked for a job. They continued to write letters and to visit one another as often as they could.

Einstein's mother had grown to dislike Mileva very much. Pauline felt that Mileva would hold her son back from pursuing his career. Pauline often tried to convince Einstein that his relationship with Mileva was wrong. When Einstein told her that he planned to marry Mileva, Pauline threw herself on her bed and sobbed, then angrily accused her son of destroying his future. Both Einstein and Mileva were stunned and hurt by his family's reaction to the relationship.

"My Little Dollie"

Einstein wrote many letters to Mileva during their separations. Sometimes he discussed his scientific ideas and thoughts in his letters, and many times he apologized for not writing to her more regularly. But he also told her how much he cared for her. He affectionately referred to her as "Dollie" and admitted that her letters made him so happy that he was teased about it. He lamented that he had not been able to kiss her in a long time and missed her terribly. He even once wrote her a poem, which ended with the words "My little Dollie's little beak/It sings so sweet and fine/And afterward I cheerfully/Close its song with mine."

A FRUSTRATING JOB SEARCH

It was traditional for students who graduated from Zurich Polytechnic to be offered entry-level assistantships with professors at the school. Usually, a graduate was hired by the professor of the field of study he or she was most interested in. In Einstein's case that was physics, but the physics professor was Heinrich Weber, the professor who was so annoyed at Einstein for addressing him as "Herr Weber." Not surprisingly, Weber did not offer Einstein a job. None of the other professors at the school offered him a position, either.

Einstein's allowance from his wealthy relatives stopped when he graduated, so he had no income. Hurt and humbled, Einstein began writing letters, asking for work. Throughout 1900 and the spring of 1901, Einstein sent letters and cards to everyone he could think of, but for months nothing came of the effort. He contacted two of his former professors, but neither of them offered him a full-time job.

Then, slowly, offers of part-time work trickled in. He worked as a substitute teacher at a technical school in Wintherthur, Switzerland. He

The World in 1900

The year 1900 was an exciting and troubling time in the world. In the United States, a terrible hurricane destroyed Galveston, Texas, killing between six thousand and eight thousand people. The Eastman Kodak Company introduced the $1 Brownie Camera, which enabled people around the world to take their own photographs. In Paris, France, the first six miles of the Paris Metro opened. In China, the Boxer Rebellion, which was an uprising against Westerners, raged.

became a tutor at a private boarding school for a time. These jobs barely paid his bills, let alone allowed him to save any money for his upcoming marriage.

What he really wanted was a job that would allow him the time and freedom to read, think, and do research into physics. But with no possibilities for getting a teaching position at a university, he had no idea if such a job existed.

EINSTEIN BECOMES A SWISS CITIZEN

Not all of the news during this time was bad. Einstein had finally relinquished his German citizenship and saved enough money to apply for his Swiss citizenship. However, he was not yet a Swiss citizen. He believed that part of the reason he was having so much trouble finding a job was that he was not a citizen of any country and that he was Jewish.

Einstein's attempts to become a Swiss citizen were problematic. In December 1900, he had to submit to an examination by government officials. They were suspicious of Einstein, so they decided to question him in person. They asked him if he drank alcohol and if he led a proper life. They also grilled him about his political beliefs. Einstein showed little knowledge or interest in world politics. Satisfied that Einstein would not be a danger to the country, the government officials accepted his application. In February 1901, he officially became a Swiss citizen.

TWO PAPERS AND UNEXPECTED NEWS

During this time Einstein never stopped studying and writing about physics. At that time scientists gained respect in the scientific community by publishing papers in scientific journals. In 1900, Einstein wrote a paper about capillarity, which is the phenomenon in which liquid rises in narrow tubes. This effect is explained by the concept of surface tension. In his paper, Einstein explored how the surface tension of water keeps water flat in a container.

Later, in 1901, he wrote a paper on thermodynamics concerning the relationship between heat and other kinds of energy. They were both published by the leading German journal for physics, showing that Einstein's ideas were important to science.

Einstein hoped that the publication of these papers would help him with finding a job. He sent his paper on thermodynamics to the University of Zurich, along with an application to the school's doctoral program. He hoped that an advanced degree would improve his chances finding a job. His application was denied by Alfred Kleiner, a professor at the school.

Throughout this frustrating job search, Einstein took every opportunity to visit Mileva. His mother was still strongly against the match. She told Albert that by the time he was thirty, Mileva, who was four years older, would be an "old hag." The stress of this rejection was difficult for the young couple, but they were determined to stay together.

Then, in 1901, Mileva discovered that she was pregnant. This unexpected news could not have come at a worse time. Einstein's father's business had collapsed again, and Einstein's temporary jobs were about to come to an end. He knew that his mother would be furious if she found out about the pregnancy.

Einstein reassured Mileva in his letters that everything would be fine as long as they worked together. He promised to stand by her. Reluctantly, he was forced to admit that he had failed in his search for a teaching job. Depressed, he looked for any work at all. He had all but given up on ever becoming a scientist and teacher.

FOUR

The Patent Office

Einstein's friends knew what a rough time he was having finding work. Einstein had sent a letter to his good friend Marcel Grossmann, who then asked his father if he could help Einstein find a job. Grossmann's father contacted a friend of his, Friedrich Haller, who was the director of the Swiss Patent Office in Bern, Switzerland. In December 1901, a job became available at the patent office, and Haller encouraged Einstein to apply for it. Some time after he applied, Einstein was informed that he had indeed been given the job of technical expert, third class, with the Patent Office. Einstein finally secured his first full-time job.

Einstein would not report to his new position until the following summer. He decided to move to Bern a few months early to establish himself in the city. Einstein found that he loved Bern. He called it an ancient and thoroughly pleasant city. He told Mileva in a letter that he planned to find them a place to live and to support himself by giving private lessons to students.

Einstein moved to Bern, Switzerland, to work in the Patent Office.

A BABY DAUGHTER FOR EINSTEIN

On February 4, 1902, Einstein found out that Mileva had given birth to their daughter, whom they named Lieserl. It had been a difficult birth, and Mileva had been too weak to write Einstein herself. Her father had written the letter instead. The fact that Mileva had not written herself frightened Einstein. He was relieved and happy to learn that Mileva and the baby were both well. Einstein wrote back, asking what his daughter looked like and how she was being fed. He also asked for a photograph or drawing of his new daughter and told Mileva that he loved her very much.

It is not clear whether Einstein's mother ever found out about her new granddaughter. The letters between Einstein and Mileva that survive do not mention anything about telling her, nor do Pauline's writings from the same time. She was still very upset that the two of them were together, and it is likely that she never learned that Mileva had had a child.

THE OLYMPIA ACADEMY

Throughout the first part of 1902, Einstein struggled to make ends meet in Bern while Mileva remained with her family. He put an ad in a Bern

Advertising for Work

When Einstein arrived in Bern, he put an ad in the newspaper advertising his tutoring services. The ad read:

"Private Lessons in Mathematics and Physics for students and pupils given most thoroughly by ALBERT EINSTEIN, holder of the fed. polyt. teacher's diploma. Trial lessons free."

newspaper, seeking students to tutor in mathematics and physics. He had hoped that he would get several eager students who would pay him enough to live until the patent office job began.

Only one person answered his ad. His name was Maurice Solovine. On the first day Solovine came to Einstein's apartment for his lesson, the two men immediately launched into a lively discussion and soon became good friends. After a short time, another one of Einstein's friends dropped by. Conrad Habicht was a mathematics scholar who was in Bern to finish training to become a teacher.

The three men agreed to meet weekly to discuss and debate science. They later named their group the Olympia Academy, after the home of the Greek gods. It was a joke because, far from being grand and rich, their Olympia Academy was poor. They often met for simple dinners of sausage, cheese, and tea, discussing politics, philosophy, physics, mathematics, and literature far into the night. Sometimes Einstein would play

Maurice Solovine was the first person to have a free lesson with Einstein.

his violin for them. They also read plays, such as the ancient Greek tragedy *Antigone*. The members of the Olympia Academy forged a friendship that lasted throughout their lives.

FIRST DAYS AT THE PATENT OFFICE

On June 23, 1902, Einstein reported for work at the Patent Office. He was one of thirteen examiners in the office and soon became friendly with his co-workers. The job of technical expert was well suited to Einstein. He was responsible for reviewing ideas for new inventions that people had submitted to the office. He compared the new ideas with existing inventions to make sure that the new ideas were original. Einstein was responsible for deciding whether the new ideas would work.

Einstein was delighted with his job. It became a game to him to figure out whether the inventions he reviewed would actually work. He quickly became very good at deciphering instructions, working out formulas, and testing the inventor's claims. He soon mastered reviewing patent claims quickly and thoroughly. The job allowed Einstein to do what he did best, which was to think and puzzle out problems his own way, in his own time, and to come up with concrete answers.

The job was also perfect for Einstein in another way. When it was slow in the office, he was able to do his own work. He had time to think about his own ideas and to work them out. But if the boss came by, Einstein hurriedly shoved his notes and equations into his desk to avoid being caught.

For the rest of his life, Einstein would love and appreciate his job at the Patent Office. Not only did it allow him the time and the freedom to think about his own ideas, but also the mental stimulation of the work helped to shape how he thought about scientific problems. He considered

Einstein spent his days at the Patent Office reviewing and analyzing inventions.

himself lucky that he never got a teaching job, which would not have given him the freedom that his "practical" job allowed. Later in life, he remembered his years at the Patent Office fondly, describing the office as a "temporal monastery" in which he developed his most wonderful ideas.

A GREAT LOSS TOUCHES EINSTEIN

By the fall of 1902, Einstein had settled into his new job and was looking forward to Mileva's arrival in Bern. He had not seen Mileva for about a year, and he had never met his daughter. His job was going well, however, and he continued to enjoy the regular meetings with his group of friends.

Then Einstein got some bad news. His father, Hermann Einstein, was dying of heart disease. Einstein immediately traveled to his family in Milan, Italy. During his father's last days, the family settled all of their old arguments about Einstein and Mileva. Hermann gave Einstein his approval to marry, and it is presumed that Pauline finally gave in, too. What should have been good news for Einstein was deeply saddened by his father's death a few days later on October 10, 1902.

Einstein had wanted very badly to be at his father's bedside when he died. However, Hermann insisted on being alone in his room at the end. This hurt Einstein deeply. He was shattered by the loss of his father. Years later he still could not think of his father's lonely death without feeling guilty. Einstein blamed himself for somehow not protecting his father from his failures in business.

Soon after Hermann's death, the grief-stricken family left Italy. Pauline moved to Germany to live with her relatives. Maja returned to school at Aarau, and Einstein returned to Bern.

A BITTERSWEET REUNION

After Einstein's return from Milan, Mileva finally joined him in Bern. They were married in a quiet civil ceremony on January 6, 1903. At the time, Einstein was twenty-three years old, and Mileva was twenty-seven. Einstein's friends, Conrad Habicht and Maurice Solovine, joined them for a wedding supper after the ceremony. The couple did not go on a honeymoon because they had no money.

Albert Einstein married Mileva Maric in a small ceremony on January 6, 1903.

When Mileva came to Bern, people noticed a change in her. She seemed unhappy, as if she carried some great sorrow. Clearly, something had happened between Einstein and Mileva, and somehow Einstein was to blame. If anyone asked her what was wrong, she would only respond that it was a personal matter. She kept Lieserl a secret throughout her life.

Mileva and Einstein got married despite this great sorrow. They believed that their love for one another was strong enough to endure life without their daughter. But it cast a shadow on their marriage that never quite went away.

What Happened to Lieserl?

When Mileva joined Einstein in Bern, she was alone. She had not brought Lieserl to Bern with her. No one knew about the baby. Even today no one knows exactly what happened to Lieserl. Some believe that Mileva gave the baby up for adoption or sent her to live with relatives. Other theories suggest that the baby might have been mentally defective, or that she died while she was still very young. The last mention of Lieserl was in a letter from 1903, when she had an illness known as scarlet fever.

In the 1930s, a woman claimed to be Einstein's long-lost daughter. When Einstein heard news of it he had the woman investigated. She turned out to be an imposter, however. To this day, the fate of baby Lieserl is still a mystery.

FIVE

1905: The Miracle Year

Things were finally going well for Einstein. He had a job he liked. He and Mileva were together, something they had worked toward for many years. He had a group of trusted friends who shared his passion for science and mathematics. And he had time to work on his own ideas.

In the fall of 1903, Conrad Habicht moved to Schaffhausen, Switzerland, and Maurice Solovine moved to Paris. By that time others had joined the Olympia Academy, such as Habicht's younger brother Paul. Einstein continued to write letters to his close friends, however, keeping the friendships alive.

On May 14, 1904, Mileva gave birth to their first son, Hans Albert. Einstein was a devoted, if somewhat distracted, father. He would sometimes rock Hans Albert's cradle with his foot while he was deep in a book. If he took the boy out for a walk in a baby carriage, Einstein

Albert and Mileva pose for a photograph with their first son, Hans Albert.

would prop his books or notes on the carriage as if it were a portable desk.

The Einsteins struggled to keep their marriage together. Mileva seemed gloomy and distracted all the time. She had dreamed of being Einstein's partner in science and in life. But she had failed the Polytechnic exam a second time while she was pregnant with Lieserl, so she had given up on having a career. Einstein still loved her, but he loved his studies too.

When friends and visitors arrived, Einstein was fun, charming, and open. When alone with Mileva, however, he usually retreated into his own world of mathematics and physics. Mileva was left to focus mainly on keeping house and raising their children. When the Olympia Academy met at their home, Mileva listened intently to the fascinating conversations, but she never joined in.

BREAKTHROUGHS THAT SHATTERED SCIENCE

Historians call 1905 the "Miracle Year" in Einstein's life because it was the year in which he wrote five very influential papers. The theories described in these papers rocked the scientific community. Each theory alone would have been enough to secure Einstein's fame as a brilliant scientist. But five, written within months of one another, was unheard of. Even more remarkable was the fact that Einstein had come to his conclusions completely on his own. He was not a professional scientist or teacher at the time. He had no university

Einstein's Ideas Shake Newtonian Science

Until the beginning of the twentieth century, the scientific world was dominated by the theories of the great seventeenth-century scientist Isaac Newton. In 1687, Sir Isaac Newton published a work titled *Philosophiae Naturalis Principia Mathematica*. In it he set forth theories that explained many physical phenomena, such as the motion of spinning objects, the motion of objects in fluids, the motion of objects through the air, pendulums, tides, gravity, and the motion of planets in their orbits around the Sun.

Newton believed that the universe was strict and orderly. All of the laws of gravity, time, and motion in the universe were absolute. The universe worked like a great clock that had been set into motion by God and left to run perfectly. Nothing would ever change. Newton's theories described what became known as the "clockwork universe."

Einstein wondered why the universe had to be so strict and orderly. He questioned why things like time, space, and matter could never change. Newton's theories did not seem able to explain these questions to Einstein's satisfaction, so Einstein started to work them out himself.

to support him. In the eyes of society at the time, he was a nobody, an unknown patent clerk.

In March of 1905, the scientific journal *Annalen der Physik* received Einstein's first paper of that year. In the paper Einstein theorized that light was made up of particles, just as Newton had thought. These particles would eventually come to be called photons. The most revolutionary part

Photoelectric Proof

It would be more than a decade before anyone could prove Einstein's theories about light particles. In 1916, an American physicist named Robert Millikan published a paper supporting Einstein's photoelectric theory. From that time on, science accepted Einstein's theories about light. Later, Einstein's theories about light particles became the basis for studying atomic and nuclear physics.

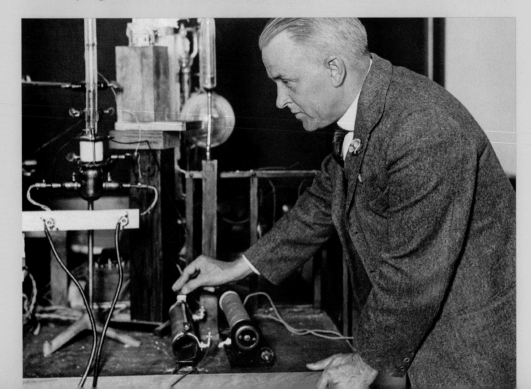

of the paper was Einstein's ideas about a phenomenon known as the photoelectric effect. The photoelectric effect is the flow of electric current in a metal when the metal is exposed to light. Although the effect itself had been known for some time, the reasons why the effect occurred baffled scientists. In this paper Einstein suggested that it was caused by the absorption of photons when light interacted with the electrons in the metal.

The journal published Einstein's paper, now known as the photoelectric paper, but few scientists noticed it. A few researchers tried to support his theories with experiments, but they were not successful.

A month later, in April 1905, Einstein sent another paper to the journal *Annalen der Physik*. It was named "A New Determination of the Sizes of Molecules." At the time the existence of atoms and molecules was debated among scientists, although Einstein was convinced that they existed. He stated that molecules existed and could be measured. Einstein calculated that a sugar molecule was about one-twentieth of a millionth of an inch across. Einstein suggested that it was possible to measure the size of molecules as they diffused in liquid, and he created an equation for determining the answer.

One Sentence Spells Success

Einstein was still hoping to earn a doctorate, or Ph.D. degree, so he sent his paper on molecules to the University of Zurich. Professor Alfred Kleiner, the same teacher who had rejected his first thesis, rejected this one too. Kleiner said it was too short. Einstein added one sentence to the paper and resubmitted it. Kleiner accepted it. Einstein was awarded his Ph.D. degree. He was always amused by the fact that he earned his Ph.D. because of a single sentence.

In May, Einstein sent his third paper to *Annalen der Physik*. This paper was inspired by the work of another scientist, Robert Brown, a Scottish botanist who lived in the mid-1800s. Brown, looking through a microscope, had dropped pollen grains into water and watched as they danced and hopped around haphazardly, as if they were alive. These movements were dubbed "Brownian movements." At the time no one knew why this happened. He suggested that the movement was caused by molecules colliding with each other. Einstein theorized that the irregular movement of the pollen occurred because liquid molecules were bumping against pollen molecules. He put forth ideas about how the movements occurred and created a mathematical formula that would calculate the pattern of movement.

THE BIGGEST BREAKTHROUGH: RELATIVITY

Einstein had been thinking a great deal about light, matter, energy, and Newtonian science in the early spring of 1905 as he was writing his paper on molecules. Then one day he woke up and he believed he had solved what he called the "cosmic jigsaw puzzle." His friend Michele Besso saw him later that day and had no idea what a momentous thing had occurred. Einstein simply greeted him by saying, "I've completely solved the problem."

In June of 1905, the paper, titled "On the Electrodynamics of Moving Bodies," was received by the editors of *Annalen der Physik*. This paper challenged Newtonian science, which had been the accepted view of the universe for two hundred years. Newton had believed that time, space, and matter were fixed and absolute. Einstein argued that time, space, and matter behaved differently under different circumstances.

Special Relativity on a Speeding Train

Until the theory of special relativity was presented, scientists had assumed that a train, and other moving objects, traveled at an absolute speed. For example, a train moving at 70 miles per hour would move at that speed no matter what objects it passed or who observed the train moving. Einstein's theory suggested that this wasn't true. The speed is only determined with respect to someone observing the train. Usually objects in space are three-dimensional and are measured by height, length, and depth. Einstein stunned the scientific world by treating time as a fourth dimension. By adding this fourth dimension, Einstein was able to create mathematical equations that described things moving in the train for both the person inside and the person outside. Now, scientists always had to look at an object's speed from a certain perspective at a particular time.

Einstein's theory is now known as special relativity. It is called "special" because it relates only to a special, or small, set of conditions, such as things that are moving at very fast and uniform speeds. It states that it is impossible to know whether something is moving or how fast it is going in an absolute way. It must be compared to a stationary object or to another moving object. In other words, one has to know how an object moves relative to, or compared to, the person observing it.

For example, to someone riding in a moving train, everything around him is at rest. But to someone on the street, everything inside the train is moving with some speed. Einstein's theory allowed scientists to calculate how things looked depending on whether a person was inside or outside the train.

Einstein wasn't finished yet, however. His theory said that the speed of an object was relative to a person observing the speed. However, the speed of light is special. It never changes. The speed of light (186,000 miles per second or 299,792 kilometers per second) is the same no matter where an observer is standing or how an observer is moving. Einstein used the speed of light in his calculations to explain how movement in time and space worked.

For many years Einstein had wondered if he could travel as fast as light itself if he could ride on a beam of light. Einstein reasoned that the light beam would then appear to be standing still relative to him. But a human could not ride on a light beam because nothing travels at the speed of light. Einstein's theory enabled scientists to accurately deal with very high speeds, such as objects traveling close to the speed of light.

In September, Einstein sent his fifth paper to the journal. This paper was only three pages long. In it Einstein continued to explain his thoughts about relativity, but he also discussed how mass and energy behave at high speeds. At the time scientists thought that mass and energy were separate characteristics of objects. Scientific theories and laws had been created to describe each one. But Einstein theorized that mass and energy were related. He wrote that an object that gave out energy would get smaller in mass. He gave a formula to measure the amount of mass that would be lost relative to the amount of energy given off.

In fact, one of his most influential discoveries was that all mass had great energy. Einstein created a formula to measure the amount of energy in a body: $E = mc^2$. The letter E represents energy. M represents mass. The c^2 stands for the square of the speed of light. This became the most famous mathematical equation in the world. This theory, and the equation that goes with it, became part of the foundation of the study of physics. Without this formula, scientists would never have figured out how to split atoms or to create atomic bombs.

Einstein's famous formula helped scientists figure out how to make the atomic bomb.

DISAPPOINTING REACTION
TO EINSTEIN'S THEORIES

Einstein expected the scientific world to take notice of his new ideas. In those days, scientists wrote letters to one another to discuss theories that had been published. Einstein's mailbox stayed empty. He did receive a few letters from scientists asking Einstein to clarify some points in his theories.

In fact, his work was not being ignored. The scientific community simply did not know what to make of it. Most scientists were baffled by Einstein's work. Some dismissed Einstein's ideas because they went against accepted scientific thought. Others simply couldn't grasp his complex scientific calculations.

Recognition of his amazing achievements would come slowly, as more scientists examined his ideas and tested his theories. However, it would take several years before other scientists were able to confirm many of Einstein's conclusions.

New Challenges

By the beginning of 1906, scientists had taken notice of Einstein's work. The great scientist Max Planck, who was the editor of *Annalen der Physik,* wrote to ask more questions about relativity. Einstein began to receive more letters about his theories.

Einstein was happy that his work had been noticed, but his personal life did not change much. He did get some good news in April 1906. At the Patent Office, he received a promotion to technical expert, second class, which included a pay raise.

EINSTEIN RETURNS TO UNIVERSITY LIFE

Einstein started thinking about his old ambition of becoming a teacher. A position at a university would give him more time to research and to

Einstein's work began to attract some attention from other scientists, such as Max Planck.

develop his ideas with other scholars. He decided to apply for the position of *privatdozent* at the University of Bern. A privatdozent was a lecturer who was not paid by the university. Instead, he taught classes and charged a small fee from each student. Holding this position was required before Einstein could become a full professor. Einstein liked the idea of becoming a privatdozent because it was a part-time position that would allow him to keep his Patent Office job.

Einstein sent all seventeen of his published papers to the University of Bern along with his application. His application was rejected because the professors who reviewed the papers insisted that he submit a unique thesis. However, Professor Kleiner, who had granted Einstein his Ph.D., had finally realized how brilliant Einstein was. He wanted Einstein eventually to teach at the University of Zurich and encouraged Einstein to apply again for the privatdozent position. Einstein did and was accepted.

Einstein began his teaching career at the University of Bern in the summer of 1908. However, his classes did not go well. His class was scheduled for 7 A.M., and only three people showed up, including his friend Michele Besso. Einstein was not well prepared for his classes. His lectures rambled, and he wore shabby clothing, a trait for which he would become known in later years. He never had more than a few students in his class. Some would stay for a time and then leave.

Throughout this time, scientists around the world had begun to discuss Einstein's theories. Letters were coming to the Einstein house in a steady stream. But no one had yet supported any of Einstein's ideas through experimentation. They were still only conjecture.

THE EINSTEINS MOVE TO ZURICH

Kleiner still wanted Einstein to be hired by the University of Zurich as a professor. However, another candidate, Friedrich Adler, had already been offered the position. When Adler heard that Einstein had also been considered for the job, he told the university that it would be absurd to give

Einstein and his family lived on this street during their time in Bern.

him the job instead of Einstein. He said the university should not lose the chance to hire a scientist as brilliant as Einstein. The university agreed and offered Einstein the position of associate professor of theoretical physics.

Einstein's longtime dream of becoming a university professor had finally come true. With regret, but also with excitement, he resigned from his job at the Patent Office in July 1909. By the fall, Einstein, Mileva, and Hans Albert had moved into an apartment in Zurich. Einstein began his new job in October 1909.

Einstein soon had second thoughts about his "dream" job. He had never liked speaking in public. He also didn't like the way professors usually conducted classes. They rarely spoke to students individually, instead lecturing from podiums. Einstein called his lectures "performances on a trapeze."

"Professor Einstein" Takes Charge

Einstein was a bad teacher at first. He hated speaking in front of a class. He rarely used his notes or stuck to the topic at hand. Gradually, however, he became more comfortable. Remembering his hatred of the rigid rules and punishments of his early school years, Einstein tried to make his lectures fun and interesting. He told jokes and entertained the students. He would stop mid-lecture to ask if they understood what he had been teaching. He told them to feel free to come to him after class for help or if they had a problem. He assured them that he would never feel disturbed, because he could always go back to his work later. His students loved him, and his classes were usually full.

Most university professors made a point of socializing with one another as a way to create alliances that might help them get promotions or other favorable rewards from the university. Einstein refused to play along with these popularity games, so he rarely socialized with the other professors at meetings or other gatherings. He angered many of his colleagues with his casual attitude toward them. He did, however, enjoy discussing scientific issues with his fellow professors.

UNHAPPY FAMILY LIFE IN ZURICH

A few other changes in Einstein's life took place when he and his family moved to Zurich. Their second son, Eduard, was born in July 28, 1910. Now Einstein had a wife, two sons, and a demanding work schedule. Living in Zurich was far more expensive than living in Bern had been, so Einstein had money worries on top of his other new responsibilities. At one point he said that his relativity theory set up a clock at every point in space, but in his reality, he couldn't afford to have a clock in his room.

The relationship between Einstein and Mileva continued to decline, although their friends were not aware of their unhappiness. Mileva had

The Einstein family grew in 1910 with the birth of Eduard. This later photograph shows Eduard, Mileva, and Hans Albert.

lost all interest in science. Einstein also began a friendship (and possibly a love relationship) with another woman during this time. Mileva found letters that had been exchanged between Einstein and the woman, Anna Schmid. Mileva's discovery stopped the correspondence, but her marriage to Einstein was already in trouble.

MORE OPPORTUNITIES, MORE MOVES

After only a few months of living in Zurich, Einstein began to think about applying for a new job. Max Planck, the former editor of *Annalen der Physik* and a respected physicist, wanted to hire Einstein as a full professor at the German University in Prague. He believed that Einstein's theory of relativity would someday be accepted as correct, making him world famous. The job would pay much more than his Zurich position, which was appealing to Einstein.

Once again, Einstein was competing for the job against another person. His name was Gustav Jaumann, and he was hired. However, Jaumann eventually rejected the offer after the university failed to meet his financial demands. Once again, Einstein was handed a job.

Mileva wasn't happy about leaving Zurich. She loved the city, and she knew that she wouldn't have any friends in Prague. Reluctantly, she agreed to move. Einstein began teaching at the German University in Prague in 1911.

By the time Einstein began teaching at the German University, more people had become aware of his theories. Newspapers ran announcements of his university appointment, which was a common practice at the time. Crowds squeezed into the lecture hall to hear him on his first day of lectures. Einstein refused to let any of this go to his head, however, arriving at the lecture wearing the same rumpled clothing.

Daily life for the family improved in Prague. Einstein's higher salary allowed them to rent a large apartment and to hire a live-in maid to help Mileva. But life also became more stressful. Einstein had to spend a great deal of time preparing for his lectures. He made time for students whenever they needed him. All of this left him little time to spend on his own ideas and theories. Einstein wished for the time and quiet that he had enjoyed while working at the Patent Office.

RESPECT FOR EINSTEIN GROWS

A short time after Einstein arrived in Prague, he was invited to speak at a scientific conference. A wealthy businessman, Ernest Solvay, was sponsoring the conference to which only a small, international group of top scientists were invited. It was a great honor for Einstein to be

The Solvay conference brought together great scientific minds from around the world. Einstein can be seen standing, second from right.

invited, and he graciously accepted. Being invited to the conference showed Einstein how well respected his ideas had become.

The people who attended the Solvay conference were among the best-known scientists in the world at that time, including Marie Curie, Ernest Rutherford, Paul Langevin, and Max Planck. The conference was a huge success, and Einstein's reputation grew.

BACK AT THE POLYTECHNIC

Einstein and Mileva did not like Prague and their marriage continued to suffer. Even their closest friends were unaware that the marriage had

Ernest Solvay

Ernest Solvay was born in Belgium in 1838. When he was very young, he was interested in physics, natural history, and chemistry. But rather than becoming a scientist, Solvay became a businessman. At the age of twenty-three, he, along with his brother Alfred, developed an industrial process to produce sodium carbonate. Sodium carbonate is used in making soap powders, glass, and paper. They founded their own business and built factories in Europe and the United States.

Solvay was concerned about social issues at a time when most wealthy businesspeople did not care about ordinary workers. In his factories, he offered pensions, paid vacations, and eight-hour workdays to his employees. He founded a number of charitable organizations and scientific institutes with his wealth. His passion for science was behind the organization of the first Solvay Congress in 1911. That first meeting was the beginning of the Solvay International Physics Council, which met twenty times between 1911 and 1991.

begun to crumble. In the spring of 1912, Einstein visited Berlin and saw a childhood friend and cousin, Elsa Löwenthal. Once Einstein returned to Prague, he began a correspondence with Elsa that eventually included declarations of love to her. It is not clear whether Mileva knew of Einstein's new affair.

By 1912, Einstein was receiving job offers from other universities. To his surprise, his former school, Zurich Polytechnic, also offered him a job. Because he and Mileva liked Zurich, he decided to accept the position.

Einstein was delighted to renew his friendship with his old friend Marcel Grossmann, who had become a mathematics professor at the university. At the time, Einstein was struggling to figure out mathematical equations that would explain how gravity worked in the universe. When he became frustrated, he would call on Grossmann, just like in the old days, and they would work on the problems together.

Later that year, Einstein got a visit from Max Planck, who was determined to lure Einstein to Berlin, Germany. He made Einstein a very generous offer. He offered him the position of theoretical physicist. He would receive a bigger salary. He would not have to lecture and would have the freedom to do his own work. He would be given a membership into the prestigious Prussian Academy of Sciences.

Einstein didn't care for the prestigious positions or the titles. He was also uneasy about returning to Germany, where he had been so unhappy as a youth. But he did like the idea of earning a bigger salary and having the opportunity to work with leading scientists. The thought of not having to lecture was also very appealing. The knowledge that Elsa lived in Berlin may also have helped him decide. By December 1913, Einstein agreed to accept the position. The family was moving to Berlin.

Over time, Einstein would become very close to Elsa and her daughters.
This later photograph shows Einstein with Elsa and her daughter Margot.

SEVEN

The Greatest Feat of Human Thinking

Einstein began his job at the Prussian Academy of Sciences in Berlin in April 1914. He was at an important point in his career. His theories were known by scientists around the world. He was on the staff of one of the most important universities in Europe. The job gave him as much time to think and study his own ideas as he wanted.

In July, only three months after the family moved to Berlin, Mileva and the boys traveled back to Zurich for vacation. Both Mileva and Einstein probably sensed that their marriage was ending. World War I broke out in Europe in August. With the beginning of the war, it became impossible for Mileva to return home. She found a room in a boarding-house for herself and the boys. Einstein promised to support his family, so he sent her most of the furnishings from the Berlin apartment and began sending her money every few months. He wrote his boys long, loving letters telling them how much he missed them. He told Hans Albert that he was sad that their separation prevented him from helping the boy study math.

Einstein, however, welcomed the quiet of the apartment and of his new bachelor life. Elsa and her two daughters, Margot and Ilse, lived close by, and they visited him often.

EINSTEIN QUIETLY REJECTS THE WAR

Einstein hoped that the war would not prevent him or his fellow scientists from doing their work. He believed that politics and science should be separate. But many of his fellow German scientists and university colleagues began working enthusiastically for the government to develop weapons. Einstein was horrified by the idea that science could be used to destroy.

Einstein was one of the few people who opposed the war from the very beginning. The war made Einstein even more dedicated to the idea of pacifism, which is opposition to violence or war to settle disputes. But Einstein rarely spoke out. The German citizens who ran the university and who paid his salary disagreed with Einstein's politics. Einstein was still a Swiss citizen, and Switzerland was a neutral country. So, instead of making political waves, Einstein chose to focus on his work instead.

LIGHT-BENDING GRAVITY

For eight years Einstein had been trying to puzzle out more questions concerning his special theory of relativity. Einstein wanted to unravel the secrets of the universe. One of the questions he was trying to solve was how gravity affected such things as light. Einstein theorized that gravity bent light. One way to see if gravity bent light was to observe how light behaved during an eclipse of the Sun. Several scientists were interested

The Great War: The War to End All Wars

What was to become the first great war of the twentieth century began on June 28, 1914. That day, Archduke Franz Ferdinand, heir to the Austro-Hungarian throne, was assassinated. As a result, the countries of Europe quickly took sides. The Allies, which included Russia, France, and Britain, faced the Central Powers, primarily Germany, Austria-Hungary, and Turkey. It is unclear even today why so many European countries scrambled to join the war so fast. Some believe it was the promise of gaining wealth and territory. Others suggest that countries honored treaties that demanded countries help one another if war was declared.

Regardless of the reasons, most believed the war would be short-lived. They were wrong. The Great War, which eventually came to be known as World War I, dragged on for four terrible years. The war marked the first time chemical weapons were used in battle. It was the first war in which airplanes bombed targets from the sky. On the ground, advanced weapons such as tanks were used for the first time. The world was horrified at the killing machine that Europe had created.

Other countries eventually joined the war. The United States entered the war on the Allied side in 1917. Armistice was finally declared on November 11, 1918. In the four years of the war, more than nine million people had died on the battlefield.

in testing Einstein's theory, but the war prevented them from traveling to places where solar eclipses were visible. For the time, his light-bending theory remained merely an idea.

THE GREATEST ADVANCE IN SCIENCE

By the fall of 1915, Einstein was still struggling to answer the questions of how gravity and the universe worked. He had been working on the problem for eight years without getting concrete results. He and his friend Grossmann had worked out complex mathematical formulas that Einstein felt sure would unlock the answer. But he had not been able to figure out how they related to one another.

This time, however, he felt like he was getting very close to the answer. For several weeks he closed his doors, ignored his mail, and focused on the problem. He skipped meals and rarely slept. Finally, the answer came. Later, he wrote that he had never worked so hard in his life, and that developing his theory of special relativity was simple in comparison.

Einstein called his new theory general relativity, and he made several breakthrough conclusions with it. One was that space has a structure, rather than being an empty nothing. He also realized that gravity was not a physical force that flew through space, pulling things together. Rather, space is curved, or warped, by the matter in space. Objects move through space not because of the pull of gravity, but by following the curves of space where it is warped near other matter or objects. This phenomena is now known as space-time curvature.

This is a very complex idea, and it is remarkable that Einstein worked it out. Einstein had proved that Newton had been wrong about how gravity worked. No other scientist had ever considered that space had a structure or that the laws of gravity that Newton had set down might be incorrect. Science had never tried to combine the principles of gravity and space to explain how the universe worked. It was a daring, creative leap of brilliance by Einstein to see that the two were somehow related, and to then figure out how.

When Einstein figured out his theory, he was thrilled. He wrote a paper titled "The Foundation of the General Theory of Relativity" and sent it to *Annalen der Physik* in March of 1916. It included all of his remarkable theories about time, space, and matter. He also published an easier-to-understand version of his theory in a book that same year.

His breakthroughs in general relativity also allowed him to solve other problems that had nagged at him. One was his light-bending theory. He had already determined that gravity bent light. Now, with his ideas about space curves, he realized that light following curves in space would be bent even farther than he had originally thought. Einstein was still hopeful that someone would test his theory by observing how light behaved during a solar eclipse.

Space and Gravity

Although Einstein's ideas are very complex, the idea of space curves can be shown with a simple diagram. Imagine that space is a sheet of rubber pulled taut. Now, place a heavy ball on the rubber sheet. The sheet will sag where the ball is lying, creating a well in the rubber. The heavier the ball, the deeper the sag. Now, roll another ball across the sheet toward the sag. The second ball will roll around and around the edge of the sag, orbiting the heavier ball. This is how Einstein believed the planets rotate around the Sun and the moon rotates around Earth.

For many years scientists had been puzzled as to why the planet Mercury's orbit fluctuated slightly. Mercury, like the other planets, orbits around the Sun in an oval-shaped path, rather than in a perfect circle. The point where Mercury is closest to the Sun during its orbit is called the perihelion. Scientists knew that, over the centuries, Mercury's perihelion changed position slowly. They called this the advance of the perihelion, but they didn't know why it occurred. They had tried to explain it but failed. Einstein used the equations he came up with for general relativity and accurately explained why Mercury's perihelion advanced.

Einstein also explained something called the red shift. Light is made up of many colors of the spectrum. Red is on one end of the spectrum, and blue is on the other. Light moving away from an observer shows the red end, while light moving toward an observer shows the blue end. Einstein predicted that distant objects in space would show the red frequency, indicating that they were moving away from the observer. Astronomers verified Einstein's red shift in 1929. Finding support for this part of general relativity showed that Newton was wrong about the idea that the universe was unchanging. It showed that objects in space are moving.

This page is part of Einstein's paper and shows the famous equation $E = mc^2$ started as $L = mc^2$.

The general relativity theory also predicted the existence of gravitational waves. Einstein believed that when heavy objects move through space, they create ripples in the space-time curve. This was the most difficult idea for scientists to test. For decades many thought it could not be

NASA Satellite to Test Einstein's Theories

The National Aeronautics and Space Administration (NASA), along with Stanford University, launched a satellite in April 2004 that may prove the existence of space-time beyond a doubt. Called Gravity Probe B, scientists have attempted to launch it since 1959.

Aboard Gravity Probe B are instruments called gyroscopes. Gyroscopes can measure the tiniest distortions in space. Scientists hope that the gyroscopes will record the space-time distortions that Einstein predicted. Gravity Probe B may also verify another idea called frame-dragging. It is the idea that bodies moving through space-time will drag space and time around themselves.

tested. However, two American scientists, Russell Hulse and Joseph Taylor Jr., were award the Nobel Prize in Physics in 1993 in part for verifying the existence of gravitational waves.

Einstein's theory of general relativity caused a sensation in the scientific world. It was described as the greatest feat of human thinking about nature and a great work of art. Although many scientists believed that Einstein's ideas were correct, none of them had been supported by experimentation. World War I was still raging, so testing scientific theories would have to wait.

THE SAD EFFECTS OF THE WAR

Einstein continued to be horrified at his German colleagues' support of the war. The strain of working with people whose ideology was so different from his own made Einstein physically ill. In addition to his work on general relativity, he also wrote several other scientific papers in 1916. The strain from all the work took its toll on his health.

Einstein finally asked Mileva for a divorce. She was so shocked and upset that she told him she had a mental breakdown. He was concerned that she had fallen ill, but he was determined to end the marriage. Their mutual friend Michele Besso became the arbitrator between Einstein and Mileva. He sympathized with Mileva's situation and tried to get Einstein to agree to a reconciliation. Einstein flatly refused, saying that living with Mileva was like having a bad smell in your nose. But he did promise Mileva that he would continue to provide for her, including giving her the prize money from the Nobel Prize, if he ever won it. He had been nominated before but had never won. Finally, Mileva agreed to the divorce.

On April 6, 1917, the United States declared war on Germany. Einstein was aghast. He called Berlin an insane asylum. His physical health got worse. He lost more than 50 pounds (22.68 kilograms). Einstein collapsed in the fall of 1917. He thought he had cancer, but doctors diagnosed a stomach ulcer and exhaustion. Elsa demanded that he move into the apartment next to hers so she could care for him more easily.

He spent the next several months in bed resting, while Elsa brought him meals. He had wanted the boys to move in with him after the divorce, but it was decided that the boys would stay with Mileva in Zurich. Einstein was especially worried about seven-year-old Eduard, who was a fragile and sickly child.

Slowly, Einstein recovered. He gained some weight and started playing his violin again. He also worked when he felt able, continuing to think about relativity and other questions about physics and the universe. In the world outside his small apartment, his ideas had begun to change scientific thought.

Headlines broke the news about the United States's entry into World War I.

EIGHT

Experiments Support Einstein's Theories

Einstein was overjoyed when the war ended in 1918. Germany had surrendered, but life in Berlin was still unstable. Germans fought in the streets for control of the country. Food was scarce.

By the beginning of 1919, Einstein was still recovering from the worst of his illness. Slowly, he began resuming his usual activities of teaching at the university and playing his violin. In February, a court in Zurich declared his divorce from Mileva to be final. A few months later, on June 2, he and Elsa were married.

Elsa, like Mileva, was a few years older than Einstein. She was an attractive woman who was protective of Einstein. She had absolutely no interest in his scientific work. Her role was to create the best possible atmosphere for Einstein to work in peace. She cooked him healthy meals, made sure he had plenty of time to study, and oversaw the upkeep of their home. Her teenaged daughters, Ilse and Margot, called Einstein "Father Einstein," and he treated them like his own daughters.

THE ECLIPSE THAT CHANGED SCIENCE

While the war was raging, it had been impossible for Einstein to visit or correspond with "enemy" scientists, that is, scientists from countries that were fighting against Germany. But scientists had been passing Einstein's general relativity paper to one another, and a growing number of them became convinced that his theories would be supported by experimental evidence.

One scientist who got his hands on Einstein's paper was British astronomer Arthur Eddington. He, along with another British astronomer named Frank Dyson, were terribly excited about Einstein's light-bending theory. They vowed to test it during the next solar eclipse, which was scheduled to occur on May 29, 1919. A solar eclipse occurs when the new moon passes directly between the Sun and Earth. The Sun appears either partially or completely covered by the moon. They planned to take pictures, through a telescope, of starlight during the eclipse. They hoped that the photographs would show light bending in the way that Einstein predicted.

However, this eclipse would not be visible in Europe or North America. Two scientific teams traveled to the two best spots on the planet to view the eclipse. Eddington and his team went to Príncipe Island off the coast of Africa. The second team went to Sobral in northern Brazil. Dyson stayed in Britain.

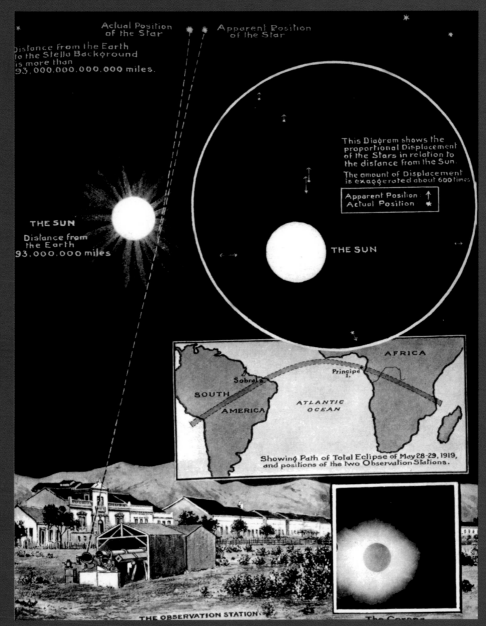

Actual Position of the Star

Apparent Position of the Star

Distance from the Earth to the Stella Background is more than 93,000,000,000,000 miles.

THE SUN
Distance from the Earth 93,000,000 miles

This Diagram shows the proportional Displacement of the Stars in relation to the distance from the Sun.

The amount of Displacement is exaggerated about 600 times.

Apparent Position ↑
Actual Position ✶

THE SUN

AFRICA

Sobral

Principe I.

SOUTH AMERICA

ATLANTIC OCEAN

Showing Path of Total Eclipse of May 28-29, 1919, and positions of the two Observation Stations.

THE OBSERVATION STATION

The Corona

This illustration shows how the light from stars is bent by the Sun's attraction.

On the day of the eclipse, Eddington woke up in Príncipe Island in the pouring rain. With so many clouds in the sky, he would be unable to see the eclipse. Eddington waited for several hours for the rain to stop. Finally, the sky cleared somewhat. Eddington frantically set up his photography equipment. When the eclipse occurred, he took as many photographs as he could before the clouds blocked his view. The second team had trouble with their main instrument, but they managed to get several good photographs anyway.

When the photographs were developed, Eddington anxiously studied them, making measurements and calculations. Frustratingly, most of the photographs were failures. But one was not. He performed his measurements on that photograph. They agreed with Einstein's theory! Later, Eddington would call that moment the greatest moment of his life.

Eddington's Journal

A passage from Eddington's journal describes the day he took the photographs that supported Einstein's light-bending theory.

"The rain stopped about noon and about 1:30. . . We began to get a glimpse of the Sun. . . . I did not see the eclipse, being too busy changing plates, except for one glance to make sure that it had begun and another half-way through to see how much cloud there was. We took sixteen photographs. They are all good of the Sun, showing a very remarkable prominence [a visible stream of glowing gas that shoots out from the Sun]; but the cloud has interfered with the star images. The last few photographs show a few images which I hope will give us what we need . . ."

Several of the second team's photographs had come out as well, further supporting Einstein's light-bending theory. Now all that Eddington and Dyson had to do was to convince the rest of the scientific world that they had evidence to support Einstein's theory.

Einstein heard of the expeditions. But it was still very difficult for him, as a resident of Berlin, to contact any scientists who lived in countries that had fought against Germany during the war. Eddington gave a preliminary report at a meeting of scientists, which was attended by a Dutch physicist who told a friend of Einstein's, Hendrik Lorentz, about the findings. Lorentz then sent Einstein a telegram sharing the good news.

FAMOUS IN AN INSTANT

Einstein was forty years old when he became famous. Although news of the discovery swept through the scientific community, the rest of the

Of Course He Was Right!

Many stories have been told about Einstein and his work. One describes how Einstein first heard the news that Eddington had gotten experimental evidence to support his light-bending theory. The story says that Einstein had received the telegram just a few days before he was meeting with a student at the university. He handed the student the paper, and she read it excitedly. Einstein answered that he already knew that the theory was correct. When the student asked him what would have happened had Eddington proved him wrong, Einstein is said to have replied, "Then I would have to be sorry for dear God. The theory *is* correct."

world would not hear about it until November 6, 1919. The first public announcement was made at a joint meeting in London of two scientific organizations, the Royal Society and the Royal Astronomical Society.

Newspapers around the world carried the story under headlines such as "Newtonian Ideas Overthrown," "Revolution in Science," and "Space Caught Bending." From that moment on, Einstein was famous

People around the world crowded together to hear Einstein's lectures. This photograph was taken during a lecture in Paris.

throughout the world. Reporters and visitors crowded his home, wanting to see the great scientist who had proven the great Isaac Newton wrong. Dozens of newspaper articles were written about him and his discovery.

EINSTEIN STRUGGLES WITH FAME

Einstein became the most famous scientist in the world. At first, he welcomed the intrusions into his life. Then the crush of reporters, well-wishers, and even those who were merely curious overwhelmed the family. Elsa began to screen everyone who came to the door, refusing entry to anyone she thought would bother Einstein. Elsa also began to sift through the bagfuls of letters, only showing certain ones to Einstein.

Einstein received invitations to visit or to lecture from universities, scientific societies, and government officials around the globe. Charities begged him to support their causes. The short book that he wrote

A Death in the Family

In 1918, Einstein learned that his mother Pauline was sick with cancer again. Several years earlier, she had been treated for the disease. By the summer of 1919, during Einstein's year of great fame, the family knew that her illness was terminal, or fatal. Einstein brought her to Berlin, where she lived with him and Elsa until her death in February 1920. Einstein was full of grief. Although he and his mother had fought a great deal, especially about Mileva, he loved her very much. He said that his mother's death made him feel like the future was hidden behind a blank wall. Elsa comforted him as best she could.

describing general relativity in simple terms sold out printing after printing. People began naming their babies "Albert." Scientific societies were named after him. Other scientists lectured about his theories, and many published books about his ideas.

The sudden attention was unnerving. He had always had trouble saying no to people, but now he found that he had to make himself refuse the hundreds of offers that poured in. He once wrote that he had dreamed that he was burning in Hell and the postman was the devil, throwing sacks full of mail at him for eternity.

Through it all, Einstein was honestly puzzled as to why he had become so famous so quickly, since he was only a scientist. He felt that he hadn't proven Newton wrong. He thought that he had only added to the tremendous work that Newton had done two hundred years before.

NINE

Einstein Faces International Fame

In the first few years that Einstein was famous, he accepted many offers to speak at universities and organizations all over the world. He was given so many honors and awards that he could not keep track of them all. His lectures were attended by thousands of people, which was a far cry from the early days when he could only get three students to listen to him lecture.

Even though Einstein was well on his way to becoming a legend, he refused to let himself be influenced by his fame. He usually carried only one rumpled suit with him when he traveled, which embarrassed some people. But that was how he had always dressed, and he wasn't about to change.

Over the years Einstein had learned to become a better speaker. He used words and phrases that everyone could understand rather than using scientific words that only a few people knew. He used simple examples to explain relativity to non-scientists. Sometimes he would play his violin to a cheering crowd.

THE DANGERS OF FAME

Einstein knew that fame gave people a measure of power. Famous people's ideas tended to carry more weight than those of people who were not famous. Einstein saw that he might do some good by speaking out against war and violence.

Germany's political situation was still very shaky after World War I. The German people wanted to hold someone responsible for the terrible

Zionism and the Jewish People

Zionism was a movement to return the Jewish people to their homeland of Israel. For centuries, the land of Israel, also known as Palestine, had been controlled by other groups. In the late nineteenth century, several organizations began to support the idea that the land should be given back to the Jews. Jewish people from around the world joined the Zionist cause. Finally, at the end of World War II, the State of Israel was created for the Jewish people. Today land in the region is still bitterly fought over between Jews and Palestinians, who had controlled the area for generations before Israel was created.

war and the destruction it caused throughout the country. They began to blame the Jews for everything that went wrong. Einstein began supporting an idea called Zionism, which was a movement to give Jewish people a homeland of their own in Palestine.

Different military groups and political organizations tried to take control of the country in the political vacuum left by the war. This created a great deal of chaos in everyday German life. There was terrible economic inflation, which made money worth less. Thousands of people were out of work, and the basics of living were hard to come by. The United States and Britain had been sending food and supplies to Germany, but many feared that this aid wouldn't be enough to allow the nation to rebound.

Throughout this period Einstein continued to maintain that peaceful negotiations were the best way to solve problems. Many people listened to him. Anti-Semites, people who are prejudiced against Jews, hated that people listened to Einstein. They accused Einstein of helping Germany lose the war because he was a well-known and outspoken

Germany was experiencing terrible inflation, which meant that it took lots of money to buy even small items. The value of paper money dropped so much that some people allowed their children to play with it.

pacifist and an opponent of German nationalism. Sometimes, he was booed during his lectures. There were rumors that Einstein's name was on a list of Jews who might be murdered.

Einstein's friends wanted him to move away from Germany, but he stubbornly refused. He was still convinced that if the German people would embrace peace, things might get better for them.

EINSTEIN CONQUERS THE UNITED STATES

In 1921, Zionist leader Chaim Weizmann approached Einstein with an idea. They wanted him to travel to the United States to raise money for their cause of creating a Jewish homeland in Palestine. He agreed, and he and Elsa set off for the United States along with Weizmann and a group of other Zionists.

Albert and Elsa Einstein traveled to the United States by ship in 1921.

Most Americans did not understand the theory of relativity, but that did not matter to them. When Einstein's ship arrived in New York Harbor, it was swarmed by huge crowds. Einstein had no idea at first that the people were there to see him. Reporters stampeded onto the ship and shouted questions at him. Unfortunately, Einstein did not speak English. Elsa struggled to translate his answers with her high-school English.

Einstein attended formal dinners and lunches with New York's government officials, including the mayor. He gave lectures and speeches throughout the city. Thousands of people squeezed into lecture halls to hear him and Weizmann speak, even though they couldn't understand German.

The group traveled the United States for three months. They were invited to Washington, D.C., where Einstein was a guest of President Warren G. Harding. They traveled on to other cities, including Boston, Chicago, and Cleveland. It was an exhausting trip for everyone. But Einstein and Weizmann had become very popular in the United States. By the end of the tour, they had raised more than $2 million for the Zionist Movement.

JAPAN CHARMS EINSTEIN

The situation for Einstein wasn't any better when he returned to Berlin from his U.S. tour. Anti-Semitism was growing. In June of 1922, German foreign minister Walter Rathenau, who was Jewish, was murdered. Einstein's friends again urged him to leave the country for his safety. He finally agreed to a six-month lecture trip to Japan and China.

In the fall of 1922, Einstein arrived in Japan. He gave many lectures and speeches, some lasting for hours. The Japanese people listened politely. They were there to see a celebrity, not to understand his complex scientific ideas. The Einsteins were introduced to the emperor and empress of Japan and were escorted on many tours of the beautiful country. Einstein was impressed by the Japanese people's manners, their intelligence, and their love of art and beauty. Einstein was very upset when he had to leave, because he had grown to love Japan so much.

The Einsteins traveled to other countries, including France and Spain. They were invited to visit Palestine, where the Zionists hoped that the new Jewish homeland would someday be created. Einstein gave several speeches supporting the Zionists' efforts.

THE HIGHEST PRIZE IS AWARDED TO EINSTEIN

When Einstein was in Japan, he received exciting news. He had won the 1921 Nobel Prize in Physics. Strangely, however, he had not won it for his ideas about special or general relativity. Instead, the Swedish Academy of Science had awarded him the prize for his light quantum theory, which he had laid out in the photoelectric paper in 1905.

The reasons for this were political. The fact that Einstein was Jewish had become a growing problem in Germany. So the committee that awarded the prize was very careful. The rules said that the Nobel Prize should be awarded for a discovery from which humankind had derived great use. No one had yet found a "use" for general relativity, but his particle light theory did have uses. In later years, the photoelectric effect would be used in such devices as solar cells and electronic cameras. The Nobel Prize was awarded for this work so that no one in Germany could argue that Einstein had received the prize unfairly.

Also problematic was the fact that Einstein was still officially a Swiss citizen, even though he lived and worked in Berlin. As soon as the prize was announced, the Swiss and German governments started fighting over which country could claim him. Switzerland pointed to the fact that Einstein had become a citizen long ago. Germany countered that he had become a German citizen when he accepted the job in Berlin.

Because Einstein was traveling in Japan when the prize was awarded, he was unable to attend the award ceremony in Stockholm, Sweden. As a compromise, the German ambassador accepted the award for him in Sweden. Then the Swiss ambassador presented it to Einstein when he returned from abroad. And, as promised, Einstein gave all the prize money to Mileva. Later, he also agreed to become a German citizen.

The rest of the 1920s were a whirlwind of travel. Einstein continued to give lectures and speeches about his theories. But he also spoke about Zionism, pacifism, and an end to violence. He was disturbed by the continued unrest in Germany. A man named Adolf Hitler was making a lot of noise in politics. His political organization, the Nazi Party, was gaining followers.

Despite his exhausting travel schedule and the unrest in Germany, Einstein still worked on his ideas and theories. He continued to fine-tune the ideas he had put forth in his general relativity and special relativity theories. He was working on a series of mathematical calculations that might combine several ideas about gravity and electromagnetism into one theory he called the unified field theory. Although he published papers about his work with the unified field theory, he never quite came up with an answer.

EINSTEIN'S HEALTH WORSENS

In 1928, while on a trip to Switzerland, Einstein collapsed. This time, a doctor diagnosed heart problems and ordered Einstein to rest in bed

Helen Dukas became an invaluable helper to Einstein. She worked for him until his death in 1955.

indefinitely. He was also forbidden to smoke his pipe. Elsa traveled to Switzerland to bring Einstein back to Berlin. There, he was cared for by Elsa and his friend, Dr. Janos Plesch.

Einstein was a model patient, obeying the doctor's orders without complaint. However, Elsa soon became exhausted with all of the work of caring for him and overseeing his business affairs. They decided to hire a secretary who could manage Einstein's heavy volume of mail, requests, lecture schedules, and other business affairs. They found a young woman named Helen Dukas. She began working for Einstein in April of 1928 and became a loyal and trusted employee and friend of the family. She remained Einstein's secretary until his death.

Einstein's Indispensable Secretary

Helen Dukas was a bright thirty-two-year-old when she began working for Einstein. At first she was terrified to meet the great scientist. But he immediately put her at ease with his gracious charm. She was very happy to learn that a knowledge of science was not required for the job. Dukas was hired on the spot.

She became his secretary, business manager, and friend. Dukas collected almost everything Einstein wrote, even digging notes out of the trash for safekeeping. When Einstein died in 1955, she and another of Einstein's friends, Otto Nathan, continued to control his papers. Some things, like his early letters to Mileva, were kept away from reporters. In the 1980s, many of Einstein's private documents were finally released. It was only then that the existence of Einstein's illegitimate daughter Lieserl was confirmed.

The Birthday Heard Around the World

Einstein turned fifty years old on March 14, 1929. His birthday became a huge event around the world. Messages, cards, and letters poured in. Important heads of state, such as U.S. president Herbert Hoover, the king of Spain, and the emperor of Japan, sent greetings. He received several violins and a sailboat from friends. But Einstein's favorite gift was a small pouch of tobacco that had come from an unemployed worker. The man had written a note that said the package included "relatively" little tobacco, but that it came from a good "field." The clever and heartfelt gift touched Einstein deeply. He wrote the man a thank-you note before he replied to any of the great world leaders.

Einstein spent almost a year recovering. During that time, Dukas proved herself to be a capable and efficient secretary. She also joined Elsa in protecting Einstein from the outside world, leaving him plenty of time to work and think. He continued to work on his unified theory. He also continued to press for peace, writing articles and speaking out against violence.

TEN

War in Germany, Asylum in the United States

By 1930, Einstein was one of the world's most popular public figures. But he still thought of himself as an ordinary person, just one who had figured out a few mathematical equations that explained natural phenomena. He did not consider his achievements to be extraordinary.

The rest of the world, however, did. His lectures and speeches were always delivered in venues that were filled to capacity. Even events concerning his work in which he did not participate drew huge crowds. For example, when the American Museum of Natural History in New York City showed a film about Einstein's theory of relativity, more than four thousand people tried to squeeze into the small theater.

The Nazis encouraged people in Germany to treat Jewish people poorly. Two soldiers hang a sign asking Germans to boycott Jewish-owned businesses on a Jewish store.

Einstein took an interest in people who were treated unfairly. If someone wrote him a letter asking for help, chances were good that Einstein would come to the person's aid. In some cases, he wrote to heads of state and important government officials who might help the individuals. Because of Einstein's stature as a world figure, he generally got what he asked for.

Einstein was especially concerned about the treatment of Jewish people in Germany. Many Jews faced constant mistreatment and discrimination because they were Jewish. The more he heard about how

Eduard's Mysterious Illness

Throughout the years, Einstein had stayed in contact with his sons, Hans Albert and Eduard. Hans Albert had grown into an intelligent and capable young man. Eduard, however, continued to show signs that he was mentally disturbed. In 1930, at age twenty, Eduard had a mental breakdown. He wrote his father several rambling, hate-filled letters, saying that he despised Einstein and that he blamed his father for abandoning the family.

Einstein went to Switzerland to see his son. After speaking to Eduard, Einstein was convinced that he did, indeed, need special help. He sent Eduard to the best doctors he could find. Even after returning to Germany, Einstein continued to be deeply worried about his younger son. Eduard was eventually diagnosed with a mental disease known as schizophrenia. Schizophrenia is a disorder that causes a separation between the thought processes and the emotions. Schizophrenics sometimes have hallucinations they confuse with reality. They display personality changes and odd behavior. Sadly, Eduard would spend most of his adulthood living in institutions.

Albert and Elsa visited Caltech several times in the 1930s. This 1931 photograph shows them with Walther Mayer, Richard C. Tolman, and F. H. Seares.

badly Jews were being treated, the more he identified with his Jewish heritage. He continued to support the Zionist effort, hoping that a Jewish homeland would become a safe haven for Jews around the world.

EINSTEIN ON TOUR

Einstein had been invited to spend the winter of 1930–1931 in Pasadena, California, at the California Institute of Technology (Caltech). There he would be a guest lecturer and would have the opportunity to spend time with scientists who had begun testing some of his theories. With the situation in Germany getting worse, Einstein agreed.

Einstein liked California. He was treated very well by the scientific community. Several scientists tried to convince him to move there permanently, but Einstein refused. However, he did agree to return to California in the future. He and Elsa returned in the winter of 1931–1932, and again in 1932–1933.

When he wasn't in California, Einstein traveled throughout Europe, lecturing and speaking at sold-out venues.

He used every opportunity to promote Zionism and to talk about his political views. Einstein spoke out about the unfair German policies against Jews. Reports of his remarks made their way back to Berlin. German government officials were not at all happy with this opinionated Jewish scientist. Elsa begged him to stop letting people know his views. Einstein refused. Elsa respected him for not giving in to fear, but she worried about his safety.

THE NAZI PARTY GAINS CONTROL

In the election of 1930, many members of the Nazi Party were elected to positions in the German government. The Nazis promised the German people that their party could bring the country out of poverty. At the time many people were still out of work and hungry. They

World-Famous Scientist Meets World-Famous Actor

During Einstein and Elsa's first visit to Pasadena, they were invited to tour several movie studios. At Universal studios, Einstein casually mentioned that he would like to meet the great silent actor Charlie Chaplin. At the time Chaplin was a superstar around the world. When Chaplin heard that Einstein wanted to meet him, he rushed to the studio for lunch. Both men were excited and honored to meet each other.

Later, Chaplin invited the Einsteins to the premiere of his movie *City Lights*. The crowd that gathered to see movie stars cheered wildly when Einstein appeared with Chaplin.

wanted to believe that better times were coming, and the Nazis promised that they were.

For the next few years Adolf Hitler delivered many mesmerizing speeches. He told the German people that their troubles had been caused by Jews, communists, and foreigners. World leaders were uneasy with Hitler's rise to power. But many believed the German people would quickly realize that Hitler was little more than a loud fanatic. However, in January of 1933, Adolf Hitler was named the chancellor, or political leader, of Germany. The Nazis were in control of the country.

THE EINSTEINS BECOME REFUGEES

Albert and Elsa Einstein left their home in Caputh, just outside Berlin, in the fall of 1932 for another stay in California. Einstein knew that things were changing in Germany. He told Elsa to take a long look at

Adolf Hitler told the German people that the Jews were to blame for all of their problems.

their home, because it would be the last time she would ever see it. Sure enough, while they were in Pasadena, word came that Hitler had been named chancellor.

Einstein and Elsa were expected to return to Berlin in 1933. However, before he left the United States, Einstein spoke out again about the rising Nazi Party in Germany. The Nazis soon heard about Einstein's remarks. They raided his summer home in Caputh, hoping to find "evidence" of Einstein's crimes against the government. Fortunately, his stepdaughter Margot had already removed his most important papers and hidden them away. The Nazis seized all of Einstein's property, declared him an enemy of the state, and offered a reward for his capture.

Einstein wasn't the only German Jew who was being attacked by the Nazis. Jewish university professors were fired, Jewish judges were removed from office, and Jewish doctors were thrown out of hospitals. The bank accounts of German Jews were seized, Jewish-owned businesses were

As the Nazi attacks on Jews increased, Einstein realized that he and Elsa could not return to Germany.

destroyed, and Jewish-owned homes were ransacked and taken by the government. It was all part of Hitler's plan to eliminate Jews from Germany.

Einstein knew that it was too dangerous for him to go home. Instead, he and Elsa stayed in Belgium while they decided where to go. In April, Elsa's daughters, Ilse and Margot, along with Dukas and Einstein's science assistant Walther Mayer, escaped Germany safely and joined them. He and Elsa renounced their German citizenships. Einstein resigned from a scientific organization he had been a member of, the Prussian Academy. The German government was happy to see him go, although many of his colleagues and friends were not.

As word spread that Einstein was then homeless, offers of asylum came in from around the world. Einstein considered several, including an invitation to live permanently in Pasadena. He finally decided to accept an invitation to work at a new scientific facility in Princeton, New Jersey, called the Institute for Advanced Study.

During his stay in Belgium, Einstein traveled to Switzerland to see Eduard. Einstein played his violin for Eduard and spent several hours with his son. He also saw Mileva, who kindly offered to let him and Elsa stay in Switzerland. Einstein was touched by the gesture but refused. He did not know it at the time, but this would be the last time he would ever see Eduard or Mileva.

Finally, Einstein was ready to leave Europe. He boarded a ship bound for the United States.

ELEVEN

Einstein at Princeton

Einstein arrived in New York in October 1933. As usual, crowds waited to greet him. But they never got to see him. Officials from Princeton University had arranged for a small boat to meet the ship before it docked and to escort Einstein's group quietly to Princeton, New Jersey.

Princeton was a lovely college town. The Institute for Advanced Study at Princeton University was founded to be a place where thinkers studying mathematics and science could work. Einstein was among the first, and certainly the most famous, scientist who accepted a position at the institute.

Einstein felt comfortable in Princeton. He explored the town and got to know its residents. Of course, everyone knew who he was, and at

The Einsteins moved to Princeton, New Jersey, and lived in this house. Albert Einstein went to work for Princeton University.

first people did not know what to expect. But they soon found Einstein to be kind and gentle. He treated everyone, even common workers, with respect. His habit of wearing rumpled clothing and of not wearing socks was considered odd but endearing. Most people respected his privacy and left him alone. Elsa also loved Princeton. She described it to a friend as one big, wonderful park.

The Einsteins eventually bought a beautiful two-story home with a nice yard and garden at 112 Mercer Street. They furnished the house with their old furniture from Germany, which the German government had allowed them to keep. Einstein built a large study on the second floor in which he could work and added more windows to the room so he would have a view of the garden.

Einstein also had an office at the Institute for Advanced Study. Each day, he walked to work. Although Einstein spoke very little English, he was learning more every day. Einstein had no obligations to teach or lecture, but he soon realized that he missed working with students. He began allowing Princeton students to come to him for help and to discuss scientific matters.

Elsa was happy to become involved in the many dinners, parties, and gatherings that the faculty and staff of the university regularly attended. Einstein, however, was just as determined not to participate in the social aspects of his new job. He didn't like the pressures of society in the United States any more than he had in Germany and Switzerland.

DEATHS IN THE FAMILY

Elsa's daughters Margot and Ilse had remained in Europe when Einstein and Elsa came to the United States. In 1934, Elsa got terrible news. Ilse

Einstein and the Paper Clip

There are many anecdotes, or stories, about Einstein. Some are humorous, like this one.

At Princeton one day Einstein needed a paper clip for some papers. He and his assistant searched his office and finally found one, but it was too bent to use. They decided to look for something that would straighten it. After opening many more drawers, they found a whole box of clips.

But instead of using one from the box, Einstein took a clip, shaped it into a tool, and then used it to straighten the bent clip! His assistant was puzzled. Why was Einstein doing this when there was whole boxful of usable clips? Einstein replied, "Once I am set on a goal, it becomes difficult to deflect me."

It is unclear whether this actually happened. But true or not, the story illustrates how single-minded Einstein could be when he was working.

had cancer and was dying. She and Margot were living in Paris, so Elsa immediately traveled to France. Elsa arrived only a few days before Ilse died. Elsa was heartbroken but glad that she had been able to see her daughter before the end.

In 1936, Elsa became very ill with liver and heart disease. Einstein was deeply focused on his work at the time and barely noticed that Elsa was ill. This made her feel lonely and neglected. She told a friend that Einstein was a wonderful husband, but that it was sometimes hard to be his wife.

Later that fall Einstein received a letter from Europe. The envelope was edged in black, indicating news of a death. His dear friend, Marcel

A Dangerous Smuggling Operation

As Elsa prepared to return to the United States from Paris, she had several trunks and boxes with her. They were filled with Einstein's books and papers that Margot and others had hidden from the Nazis. Getting them to the United States would be dangerous. Elsa was not a U.S. citizen. If she was caught smuggling such documents, it could cause an international incident between the United States and Germany. She could be imprisoned or, worse, sent back to Germany.

Luckily, the Blackwoods, friends of the Einsteins from Princeton, were traveling aboard the same ship as Elsa. They agreed to help. When the ship docked in New York, Mr. Blackwood told the authorities that the trunks and boxes were his. He wasn't questioned, and the documents arrived safely. Eventually these papers became an important part of the Einstein Archives, an organization dedicated to preserving Einstein's papers and materials.

Grossmann, had died on September 7. He wrote a heartfelt letter to Grossmann's widow, telling her how much her husband had meant to him.

In the letter he recalled what a good student Grossmann had been, while Einstein had been a dreamer. He cherished the memories of their student days, drinking iced coffee at cafés and having lively discussions. He wrote that if it hadn't been for Grossmann, he would never have gotten the job at the Patent Office. He also said that it was a beautiful thing that he and Grossman had been friends all of their lives.

By then it was clear, even to Einstein, that Elsa was gravely ill. That winter, she got worse. Einstein put away his books and papers and stayed with Elsa day and night. He sat by her bedside and read to her. They talked a great deal. She died on December 20, 1936.

Two people whom Einstein had loved deeply had died in a short period of time. Einstein was terribly upset. His friends suggested that he take a break from work. Einstein refused, saying that he needed his work more than ever. Margot, who had nursed her mother for months, was devastated. She soon moved in with her stepfather at 112 Mercer Street. Helen Dukas took over housekeeping duties and continued to be Einstein's secretary. Three years later, in 1939, Einstein's sister Maja came for a visit and decided to stay in the United States. Einstein was surrounded by family, friends, and his work.

HELP FOR DESPERATE REFUGEES

Throughout the 1930s, the situation for Jews living in Germany and in other parts of Europe had grown steadily worse. Einstein received letters from friends and acquaintances trapped in Europe asking for help to escape.

Thousands of Jews were forced to go to concentration camps by the Nazis.

Einstein stopped speaking out against Hitler, because he was afraid that it might hurt the Jews living in Europe. Hitler and the Nazi Party had Jewish Germans living in a stranglehold of fear and intimidation. Jewish people lost their jobs. Thousands were rounded up and forced to live in ghettos. Their homes and businesses were destroyed. Einstein decided to help Jews secretly escape from this terror. Einstein's method was to sponsor Jews entering the country by signing documents and putting a little money aside for the refugees when they arrived. At times, he asked close friends to help him. Einstein eventually managed to help several Jews escape to the United States.

One young man he helped to escape was Boris Schwarz. Schwarz had played violin with Einstein when he was younger, and they had remained friends for years. To help Schwarz escape, Einstein signed a document that promised he would support Schwarz if the United States allowed him to enter. At first officials denied Schwarz's request because the document wasn't enough proof that he actually knew the great scientist. Then Schwarz showed them an autographed photograph of himself and Einstein. He was allowed to leave.

The horror in Germany grew steadily worse. On the night of November 9, 1938, Hitler ordered his armies to storm through Germany and Austria, which was under German control, and to kill or capture all the Jews they could find. The soldiers destroyed Jewish synagogues and hospitals. Hundreds of Jews were killed. Thousands more were forced onto trucks and taken to prisons or to concentration camps. The night was called *Kristallnacht* ("Crystal Night") after the countless broken windows whose glass littered the streets. The world was horrified at the Nazi's brutality.

EINSTEIN QUESTIONS PACIFISM

World War II began in Europe in 1939, several months after Kristallnacht, with the German invasion of Poland. Soon after, France, Great Britain, Australia, and several other countries declared war on Germany. However, as the situation in Europe grew worse, Einstein began to question whether pacifism was effective. Maybe, Einstein thought, there were some cases in which people needed to fight. He worried that the pacifist views of others in Europe actually created the opportunity for Hitler to gain power. Reluctantly, he decided that it was better to fight Hitler and the Nazis than to cling to his pacifist ideals.

Some people saw Einstein's change of heart as a betrayal. At the time, many people in the United States also believed in pacifism. They didn't want the United States to become involved in a European war. But most Americans had no idea how bad it had become for Jews living in Europe. They did not yet know about Hitler's concentration camps or that Jews and other minorities were being murdered by the thousands.

A NEW THREAT TO THE WORLD

German scientists, using Einstein's $E = mc^2$ formula, had begun experiments to try and split atoms, thereby releasing a great amount of energy. It looked as if the Germans might discover how to make an atomic bomb. However, many of the scientists working on the task were Jewish. Several of them fled Germany, taking their knowledge of the atom's capability with them. But the danger was still very real that the Germans might develop a weapon that would allow them to conquer the world.

Einstein had not believed that these kinds of terrible weapons would be invented in his lifetime. In July 1939, he was visited by a friend, Leo Szilard, a physicist from Hungary. Szilard was very worried that the Germans might develop the atomic bomb. He told Einstein about the German experiments. They agreed that the U.S. government

Albert Einstein and Leo Szilard reenact the signing of the letter they sent to President Roosevelt years earlier.

should be made aware of these new developments. Einstein agreed to write a letter to Franklin Roosevelt, the president of the United States.

Szilard gave the letter to his friend Alexander Sachs, who took it to the president personally in October 1939. Roosevelt agreed to hear

Einstein's Letter to President Roosevelt

The letter that Einstein wrote to President Roosevelt has become one of the world's most famous documents. It reads, in part:

It may become possible to set up a nuclear chain reaction in a large mass of uranium, by which vast amounts of power and large quantities of new radium-like elements would be generated. Now it appears almost certain that this could be achieved in the immediate future.

This new phenomenon would also lead to the construction of bombs, and it is conceivable—though much less certain—that extremely powerful bombs of a new type may thus be constructed. A single bomb of this type, carried by boat and exploded in a port, might very well destroy the whole port together with some of the surrounding territory. . . . In view of this situation you may think it desirable to have some permanent contact maintained between the Administration and the group of physicists working on chain reactions in America. . . .

Yours very truly,
Albert Einstein

what Sachs had to say, so Sachs read the letter to the president. The president was persuaded. Later President Roosevelt wrote a thank-you letter to Einstein, telling him that he had decided to take action.

The president created a committee that launched a secret project to develop the atomic bomb. The project, known as the Manhattan Project, was eventually successful in creating the world's first atomic bomb. Einstein did not participate in the Manhattan Project, although he knew that it existed.

EINSTEIN BECOMES A U.S. CITIZEN

As the war in Europe escalated in the late 1930s, Einstein realized that he could never return home. He had grown to love his adopted home, the United States, so he decided to become a U.S. citizen. Margot and Helen Dukas also decided to become citizens. They filled out the necessary papers and waited for them to be approved. Government officials offered to speed up his application, but Einstein said that he was happy to wait just like everyone else.

Einstein takes the oath of citizenship and becomes an official U.S. citizen in 1940. Beside him are Margot and Helen Dukas.

On October 1, 1940, seven years after Einstein settled in Princeton, he took the oath of U.S. citizenship. Beside him were Margot and Helen. Only fourteen months later, on December 7, 1941, the Japanese attacked Pearl Harbor, and the United States entered World War II.

WORLD WAR II AND THE ATOMIC BOMB

The terrible war raged for four more years. Germany, Japan, Italy, along with several other countries, fought the Allies, which included the United States, Great Britain, the Soviet Union and France, among other countries. Armies battled across Europe and islands in the Pacific Ocean. Thousands of cities and towns were destroyed by bombs.

Throughout the war, Einstein continued to help as many Jews escape Europe as he could. For instance, he got a letter from a relative, Brigitte Alexander-Katz, who was desperately trying to escape Europe with her baby boy. When Einstein heard that she had survived Hitler's soldiers and was trying to get into Mexico, he wrote a letter vouching for her and offering to recommend her to the Mexican authorities.

By 1945, it became clear that the Germans were going to lose the war. Europe was in shambles. Millions of Jews and other minorities had been killed by the Nazis in extermination camps. The U.S. government had been successful in developing the atomic bomb. Germany surrendered in May 1945, but several other countries, including Japan, still fought on. It was decided to drop the atomic bomb on Japan, with the hope that it would end the war quickly.

Einstein was afraid that using the bomb would be a terrible mistake. He wrote another letter to President Roosevelt, but the president died before it reached him. The new president, Harry Truman, was determined to end the war by using this new weapon.

On August 6, 1945, an atomic bomb was dropped on the Japanese city of Hiroshima. A second bomb was dropped on Nagasaki three days later. Einstein, who was on vacation, heard the sad news on the radio. He had once visited Japan and had loved the country and its people. Soon after the bombs were dropped, Japan surrendered and World War II ended.

Word spread about Einstein's role in the development of the atomic bomb and his misgivings about using it. To many people, he became a symbol of the horrors of war, because he created the theory that enabled scientists to make the bomb. For others, however, he was a sympathetic and brave man who spoke out against the destruction that he helped cause. He spent the rest of his life speaking out against nuclear warfare.

TWELVE

Later Years

Einstein retired from the Institute for Advanced Study in 1945. He still used his office there to work on his physics theories, but other business took up much of his time. He was given many awards and honors. He still gave lectures and speeches, but he was slowing down. He still enjoyed playing his violin.

The dream of establishing the Jewish homeland that he and other Zionists had worked so hard for finally came true with the creation of the State of Israel in 1948. However, there were many problems with the agreement. Many Arabs who already lived in Palestine were upset over giving up their land. Many Jews felt that they deserved more land than they were offered because of the horrible toll that the war had taken on them. The conflicts between Arabs and Jews over land and resources in the Middle East continue today.

PRIVATE LIFE, PUBLIC FIGURE

In 1948, Einstein got the sad news that Mileva had died in Zurich. Then it was up to Einstein to care for his son Eduard, who still lived in a mental hospital. He made sure that Eduard's hospital bills were paid and hired a guardian for his son. Hans Albert had immigrated to the United States several years before and had become a successful scientist in his own right.

Einstein was seventy years old in 1949. He still worked when he felt up to it, but he spent most of his time strolling through his Princeton neighborhood and visiting with friends.

Einstein's beloved sister Maja suffered a stroke after the war. Einstein spent time reading and talking with her, just as he had done with Elsa when she had been ill. Maja died in 1951.

Until the end of his life, Einstein received honors from around the world. In 1952, he was offered the position of president of Israel, but he

Is This Picture Real?

One of the most famous photographs of Einstein shows him playfully sticking out his tongue at the camera. But is it real? Indeed it is. It was taken on March 14, 1951, by an unknown photographer. It was Einstein's birthday. All day he was being asked to smile for the camera. Finally, he got tired of smiling and stuck out his tongue instead.

declined. In 1955, many scientific organizations invited him to their fiftieth anniversary celebrations of his 1905 work. Unfortunately, by that time his health was failing and he could not attend.

Despite his failing health, Einstein continued to speak out strongly for causes he believed in. He never forgave the German people for their treatment of the Jews. When he was asked to rejoin the Bavarian Academy, he declined, saying in a strongly worded letter that he compared the behavior of German scientists to that of a mob and that he would never be a part of German life again.

He also spoke out against the use of the atomic bomb. Einstein realized that the world would never be the same again, and that as long as the world had the bomb, no one was safe.

By 1955, Einstein's health was failing rapidly. Several years before he had been hospitalized with stomach pains, and doctors had operated on him twice. He was depressed that he had never been able to finalize his

In his final years, Einstein worked on his unified field theory.

unified field theory. He had spent the last several years working hard on the answer, but now he felt that the time may have been wasted. He also felt guilty about his role in creating the atomic bomb. He once told a friend that his biggest regret was sending the letter to President Roosevelt, although he knew that he had done it to stop Germany from creating the bomb first.

In April, Einstein began having terrible stomach pains and collapsed. Doctors thought that another operation might help him, but he refused it. He had already made arrangements for his death. A few days later he agreed to go to the hospital. Margot and Hans Albert came to see him. He died on April 18, 1955.

Einstein had been very clear on what he wanted his family to do upon his death. He asked for no funeral, grave, or monument. He wanted to be cremated. His family followed his wishes.

EINSTEIN'S LEGACY

Einstein's scientific work changed everything people had once believed about how the universe worked. Since he published his theories in 1905,

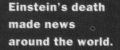

Einstein's death made news around the world.

scientists have been trying to prove them. Some may never be proven. But Einstein looked at scientific problems in new and creative ways. He inspired scientists to look at science from many different points of view. Because of him, our understanding of the world and the universe is much greater.

His scientific ideas paved the way for the creation of thousands of everyday objects. Television cameras, fiber-optic cable networks, power generators, calculators, manufacturing processes, and even computers were developed in part by using Einstein's theories.

His beliefs also influenced a great many people. He was not afraid of speaking out about things he believed in, even if his words put him in danger. In part because of his work, the State of Israel was created and the Hebrew University of Jerusalem was completed. Jewish people who might have been killed by the Nazis were saved. Some people might not have agreed with Einstein's ideas, but many respected him for speaking

Einstein's Brain

One of Einstein's requests was that his brain be used for research. Before he was cremated, Dr. Thomas Harvey removed Einstein's brain. He planned to study it to see if it was any different from other brains. Harvey cut the brain into several pieces and put them in two large glass jars.

For many years Harvey kept Einstein's brain with him at his home or office. He once stored the two jars in his basement. He sent samples of Einstein's brain to other scientists, and a few scientific papers were written about it. In 1996, Harvey gave the remaining parts of Einstein's brain to Dr. Elliot Krauss, the chief pathologist at Princeton Hospital.

The Hebrew University of Jerusalem is part of Einstein's legacy. It is through his efforts that the university was completed.

out about them so strongly. At the end of his life, he was revered as a man of peace for his opposition to nuclear war.

However, Einstein's greatest legacy is himself. Throughout his life, he conducted himself with dignity. He treated everyone with respect. He never let his fame overwhelm him. People who met him were constantly amazed at his kindness, which they did not expect from such a famous person. Einstein's greatness came from inside.

Timeline

ALBERT EINSTEIN'S LIFE   WORLD EVENTS

1879 Einstein is born in Ulm, Germany, on March 14.

1880 The Einstein family moves to Munich, Germany.

1881 Einstein's sister Maja is born.

1894 The family moves to Italy, leaving Einstein behind to finish school.

1895 Einstein fails the entrance exam for Zurich Polytechnic and begins high school in Aarau, Switzerland.

1896 Einstein graduates from Aarau and enrolls at Zurich Polytechnic.

1900 Einstein graduates from Zurich Polytechnic.

1901 Mileva becomes pregnant, and Einstein is granted his Swiss citizenship.

1902 Mileva and Einstein's daughter Lieserl is born, and Einstein begins working at the patent office. He and two friends form what is later known as the Olympia Academy.

1903 Einstein and Mileva get married.

1904 Einstein's son Hans Albert is born on May 14.

1905 This year Einstein publishes five influential scientific papers, including ones on the photoelectric effect and special relativity. He is awarded a Ph.D. from the University of Zurich.

1907 Einstein develops the equation $E = mc^2$.

1908 Einstein accepts the job of privatdozent.

1909 Einstein resigns from the Patent Office and becomes an associate professor at the University of Zurich.

1910 Einstein's second son Eduard is born on July 28.

1911 Einstein becomes a full professor at the German University in Prague.

1912 Einstein accepts a professorship at Zurich Polytechnic.

1914 Einstein and Mileva separate. Einstein becomes a member of the Prussian Academy of Sciences.

World War I begins.

1915 Einstein completes his general theory of relativity.

1916 The paper on general relativity is published.

1918 World War I ends.

1919 Einstein divorces Mileva and marries his cousin Elsa Löwenthal. In South America, British astronomer Arthur Eddington takes photographs of an eclipse that support Einstein's light-bending theory.

1921 Einstein tours the United States to raise money for the Zionist Movement.

1922 During a tour of Japan, Einstein is notified that he has been awarded the 1921 Nobel Prize in Physics.

1929 Einstein collapses from exhaustion.

1930 Einstein and Elsa visit Pasadena, California, and the California Institute of Technology for several months.

1933 The Nazis ransack and seize Einstein's property in Germany. Einstein accepts an offer to work at the Institute for Advanced Study in Princeton, New Jersey.

Adolf Hitler is appointed chancellor of Germany.

1934 Ilse, Einstein's stepdaughter, dies of cancer in Paris.

1936 Einstein's friend Marcel Grossman and Einstein's wife, Elsa, die.

1938 Kristallnacht (Crystal Night) occurs.

1939 Einstein writes a letter to President Roosevelt about the nuclear threat. Einstein's sister, Maja, arrives in Princeton.

Germany invades Poland, and World War II begins.

1940 Einstein, Helen Dukas, and his stepdaughter Margot becomes U.S. citizens.

1941 The Japanese attack Pearl Harbor, and the United States enters World War II on the Allied side.

1945 The United States drops atomic bombs on Japan, ending World War II.

1948 Mileva dies.

1951 Maja dies.

1952 Einstein declines an offer to become president of Israel.

1955 Einstein dies on April 18 at a hospital in Princeton, New Jersey, at the age of seventy-six.

To Find Out More

BOOKS

Brallier, Jess. *Who Was Albert Einstein?* New York: Grosset & Dunlap, 2002.

Calaprice, Alice, editor. *Dear Professor Einstein: Albert Einstein's Letters to and From Children.* Amherst, NY: Prometheus Books, 2002.

MacLeod, Elizabeth. *Albert Einstein: A Life of Genius.* Tonawanda, NY: Kids Can Press, 2003.

Oxlade, Chris. *Albert Einstein.* Orlando, FL: Raintree/Steck Vaughn, 2003.

Schaefer, Lola and Wyatt Schaefer. *Albert Einstein.* Bloomington, MN: Pebble Books, 2003.

Swisher, Clarice. *The Importance of Albert Einstein.* San Diego, CA: Lucent Books, 1994.

ORGANIZATIONS AND ONLINE SITES

Albert Einstein Archives
http://www.albert-einstein.org/

This site, maintained by the Hebrew University in Jerusalem and the Jewish National and University Library, is an extensive Web site devoted to Einstein's life and his writings.

Allworld Knowledge: Isaac Newton's Laws
http://www.allworldknowledge.com/newton/

Isaac Newton's laws of motion are explained on this easy-to-understand Web site.

Einstein Archives Online
http://www.alberteinstein.info

This site, a joint project between the Hebrew University of Jerusalem and the Einstein Papers project at CalTech in California, offers online access to some of Einstein's professional and personal papers and writings.

Einstein Exhibition for Kids
http://www.albert-einstein.org/start.html

This fun site includes images of drawings and letters that Einstein received.

Gravity Probe B
http://einstein.stanford.edu

This site provides up-to-date information on the NASA/Stanford space project, Gravity Probe B. This satellite is designed to verify Einstein's space-time theory.

Institute for Advanced Study
http://www.ias.edu/

This site includes the history and purpose of the institute at which Einstein worked for twenty years.

Museum of Natural History
Online Einstein Exhibit
http://www.amnh.org/exhibitions/einstein/energy/special.php

This site is part of an exhibit showcasing Einstein's theory of special relativity. It also contains information about his other scientific theories and his life.

Nobel Prize Foundation
http://www.nobel.se/physics/laureates/1921/

Included on this site is a biography of Einstein that focuses on his scientific work on the photoelectric theory.

NOVA Online
Einstein Revealed: Time Traveler Game
http://www.pbs.org/wgbh/nova/einstein/hotsciencetwin/index.html

Part of a NOVA site devoted to Einstein's theories, this page explains elements of the theory of relativity through an interactive game.

A Note on Sources

Hundreds of books and articles have been written about both Einstein's life and his remarkable scientific theories. Einstein wrote several himself, including *Autobiographical Notes*, *Ideas and Opinions*, and *Out of My Later Years*.

There are several excellent biographies of Einstein, including Denis Brian's *Einstein: A Life*; Philipp Frank's *Einstein: His Life and Times*; *Einstein* by Michael White and John Gribbin; and *Albert Einstein* by Albrecht Fölsing. Einstein's secretary, Helen Dukas, co-wrote a biography of Einstein titled *Albert Einstein: The Human Side* in 1979. It includes the text of letters he wrote, but little biographical information.

Dukas controlled most of Einstein's papers and documents until her death in 1982. Prior to that, she rarely allowed journalists access to most of them. Books written after her death include more in-depth information about Einstein's personal life.

—*Allison Lassieur*

Index

About the Author

Allison Lassieur has written more than fifty books about famous figures, history, world cultures, current events, science, and health. In addition to writing, Lassieur studies medieval textile history. She lives in Pennsylvania in a one-hundred-year-old house with her husband Charles.